MEETING PRACTICE
and
PROCEDURE
for
BUSINESS
CORPORATIONS:
BOARDS
and
SHAREHOLDERS

HARRY S. ROSENTHAL

Print ISBN: 978-1-09832-541-1

eBook ISBN: 978-1-09832-542-8

Parliamentary Services Publishing

DISCLAIMER

This publication is intended to provide accurate and authoritative information on the subject matter discussed. All information found in this publication is general in nature and based on the experience and research of the author. The analysis is to be considered the opinion of the author.

This reference is offered and sold with the understanding that the publisher and author are not engaged in rendering legal, parliamentary or other professional service in specific situations. This publication should not be used as a substitute for obtaining professional service or in lieu of seeking legal or parliamentary advice in specific situations. All the information contained in this text has been researched for accuracy; however, neither the author nor the publisher may or can be held liable for errors, omissions, misuse or misinterpretation. The author and publisher make no representations or warranties as to the accuracy of any information.

Statutory and case law in each state differ and change over time. In addition, organizations use, apply, and rely on differing rules. Each situation is unique and must be individually researched by a qualified professional. The reader is urged to consult with an appropriate licensed and qualified professional before taking any action that might involve any interpretation or application of information within the realm of a licensed or certified professional practice.

The author and publisher make no representations or warranties as to the accuracy of any information contained in the book, including any warranties of merchantability or fitness for a particular purpose. In no event shall the author or publisher have any liability to any party for special, incidental, tort, or consequential damages arising out of or in connection with the book, even if the author or publisher has been advised of the possibility of such damages.

ACKNOWLEDGMENTS

I wish to thank my wife, Lynn, for her ongoing support and encouragement throughout the research and writing of this book.

I also gratefully recognize and especially thank Nancy Kozlowski for her excellent and tireless secretarial work, patience, and insightful comments during this project.

Special thanks to Liz Seif and Terra Lane for their outstanding technical assistance and expertise.

Thank you to Ryan Rosenthal and Alex Rosenthal for their comments. And special thanks for the inspiration from my grandchildren.

CONTENTS

Introduction

Business corporations conduct their board and shareholder meetings using procedures obtained from and required by various sources. These procedures, especially those that are required, are affected or determined by applicable state statutes or federal requirements. Common (case) law also affects these procedures. The purpose of this book is to present information about how these meeting procedures may apply to U. S. business corporations. Selected case law that interprets or applies these procedures is included.

Each situation differs and must be individually researched and evaluated. This includes statutory and case law and the facts involved in the particular situation.

Nonprofits, in contrast with business corporations, rely heavily on parliamentary reference books, especially *Robert's Rules of Order*. *Robert's Rules* originated or refined many of the meeting rules and concepts for nonprofits, beginning in the early 1900s. It, and other reference books like it, have been updated and revised over the years. Many of underlying rules and procedures contained in the nonprofit reference texts are used by business corporations in their meetings.

One common denominator is that both nonprofit and business corporation meetings are motion driven. Most motions require a majority vote for the matter under consideration to be adopted.

Having an understanding of the procedural rules for nonprofit meetings can shed light and perspective on those for business corporation meetings. Many of the same rules apply to both types of organizations. For example, the parliamentary references for nonprofits set out specific procedures for the holding of an executive (secret) session. Business corporations, where permitted, have followed suit by conducting all or parts of certain board and committee meetings (such as those of a compensation committee) in executive session. Another example is that business corporations consider a tie vote a rejection of a motion or proposal, just as nonprofits do.

It should be noted that the role and concepts of the two parliamentary references for nonprofits are included in this book to provide background and context. However, they are typically not binding in their entirety in for-profit corporate meetings – unless so adopted or otherwise recognized by or for the organization.

Other situations illustrate significant differences between nonprofit parliamentary rules and the meeting rules used by business corporations. These differences are often explainable by statutory or case law that does not apply to nonprofits. For example, nonprofits ignore abstentions when tabulating a vote count. In the case of for-profits, abstentions are sometimes (but not always) counted as "no" votes. When an abstention is counted as a "no" vote, passage of a measure is more difficult because more affirmative votes are needed. That higher bar for passage does not affect nonprofits when they follow the parliamentary references.

Occasionally, a court cites *Robert's Rules* for background information or support in explaining a corporate legal decision arising from a meeting. However, most times courts may ignore, discount, or reject it altogether in favor of more traditional legal authority.

The meeting rules for business corporations are in order of legal authority the following:

1. applicable statute (most)
2. applicable case law
3. parliamentary references such as *Robert's Rules* (least)

Two of the most prominent parliamentary references used by non-profits today are *Robert's Rules of Order, Newly Revised 12th Edition* (*RONR*) and the *American Institute of Parliamentarians Standard Code of Parliamentary Procedure* (*Standard Code*). (A new edition of the *Standard Code* is anticipated for publication in 2022. References in the footnotes to *Robert's Rules* refer to paragraph numbers and not page numbers. The reader should refer to this edition for any applicable changes.) These are the two references for nonprofits referred to in this book. As noted, some nonprofit procedures also apply to business corporations and others do not. The two nonprofit texts illustrate important principles and are noted throughout the book.

While shareholder agreements and LLCs and other business entities are occasionally mentioned, meeting procedures used by traditional U.S. business corporations are the primary subject of this book.

CHAPTER 1

Presiding Officers, Meeting Rules, and Selected Parliamentary Procedures

§ 1 Presiding Officers

Usually, the president of a business organization or the board chairperson (often the same person) runs the board or shareholders business meeting. This is commonly stated in the bylaws or other formal organization policy. However, absent an applicable provision in the corporate documents or a statute, it is not formally required. Whoever runs the meeting should be competent to do so. Sometimes an organization will hire a professional presider, perhaps a professional parliamentarian, to conduct the meeting. "There also may be times when it may be advantageous for the parliamentarian to preside over the business portion of a meeting or convention, or when a part of a meeting may be controversial and the assembly would welcome a neutral party to preside. This can be pre-arranged, but it still requires permission from the assembly."[1] A professional parliamentarian can also be hired to sit next to or near the chair during a meeting to help as needed. The parliamentarian is only an advisor to the chair and makes no final decisions.

A commonly used bylaw that featured in an Indiana case described the role of the president as including presiding at all meetings of the shareholders and directors.[2] In a Kentucky case, it was noted that a similar internal corporate regulation stated, "The President shall preside at all meetings of shareholders and discharge all the duties that devolve upon a presiding officer . . . ."[3]

A presiding officer should have the skills to—among other things—ensure that all attendees understand the proposals offered at a meeting, prevent improper conduct, prevent the use of dilatory tactics, and know and be able to apply parliamentary procedure fairly.[4]

AGENDA

An agenda should be established that sets the order and content of a business meeting.[5] This agenda may be mandated by the organization's documents or voted upon at the beginning of the meeting. Often, leadership drafts the preliminary agenda. Under *Robert's Rules*, the agenda may first be approved by a majority vote and it may be changed during the meeting by a two-thirds vote. Matters of importance should be scheduled to be addressed early in a meeting so there is enough time to get to them. The agenda can have an impact when there is a disagreement about a meeting. For example, in a 2015 Massachusetts case,[6] the court looked at the agenda to see if a disputed subject had been discussed.

SELECTING A CHAIR

Since the chair exerts considerable influence over the direction and outcome of a meeting, it is no surprise that there is considerable case law on selecting a meeting chair. As noted above, the bylaws typically identify the board meeting chair, usually the president. There may be more options and shareholder control over who chairs at a shareholders meeting.

The shareholders' option to select a chair is illustrated in a 1995 Texas case.[7] The case featured a dispute about who had the right to preside over a shareholders meeting. The corporate bylaw provided, "Unless some other person or persons are elected by a vote of the majority of the shares then entitled to vote at a meeting of shareholders, the President shall preside and the Secretary shall prepare minutes of each meeting of shareholders."[8]

A 2007 California case illustrates that not everyone who presides at a shareholders meeting has to be an officer.[9] This was consistent with the past practice of the corporation, which had no bylaw detailing the manner of selection of the chair. The court looked at a corporate bylaw that used the term "presiding officer" and noted that it "does not mean that everyone who ever presides at a shareholders meeting (and thus serves as a "presiding officer") thereby becomes an officer of [the corporation]."[10]

An appellate court in New York noted the absence of detail in the written procedure for selecting a meeting chair. The court found no error with the board of directors designating a director of the company to chair of the annual shareholders meeting.[11]

In this writer's opinion, who chairs a shareholders' meeting gives rise to more controversy than who chairs a board meeting does.

COURT APPOINTMENT OF CHAIR
Disputes about who is to preside may wind up in court. Examples follow.

A 2012 Guam case relied on a statute providing that "the judge of the Superior Court" may direct the person calling the meeting to preside in order to resolve a dispute that occurred before a shareholders' meeting had been called.[12]

In a Delaware case involving a board being deadlocked, a custodian was appointed by the court.[13] Among other duties, the custodian set the agenda of the board meetings, fully presided, and oversaw the discussion.

CHANGING A CHAIR
Attempting to change a meeting chair sometimes creates controversy. *Robert's Rules* provides a procedure to temporarily replace a

chair with another presiding officer if the chair "culpably fails to perform the duties of the chair properly in a meeting."[14]

The courts lean to allowing shareholders latitude in deciding who is to chair their meetings. This is illustrated by the following legal cases.

The *ITC Cellular* court, finding against the actions of the president in running the shareholders meeting and commenting on someone else taking the chair, stated:

> The President, however, cannot thwart the will of the majority by refusing to allow an election of a new chairperson as provided for in the bylaws of the corporation. Because the president defaulted by failing to take charge of the meeting, it was not fatal for someone else to temporarily conduct the meeting until a presiding officer could be elected.[15]

A 1974 Pennsylvania federal district court looked at who should preside at a bank's annual shareholders meeting.[16] The court found that the shareholders and proxy holders for the majority of shares represented at the annual meeting were denied their right to elect the chairman of the meeting. At first, the president of the bank chaired the meeting. Certain shareholders objected. A motion was made and seconded for the shareholders to elect the meeting chair. The bank president ruled the motion out of order. The motion was presented a second time and was again ruled out of order. According to minutes in the bank's records, from 1960 to 1968 the chair was "chosen" and from 1969 to 1973 the chair was "elected."[17]

A New York case involved a corporation's president who allegedly denied shareholders their rights when he, presiding over a shareholders meeting, unilaterally adjourned the meeting.[18] With a quorum still present, the shareholders, by motion, elected a new chair.[19]

An election of directors then ensued. The court upheld the election and found that the president did not have the right to declare the meeting adjourned.[20] The court stated that "[i]t is the shareholders' meeting, the owners of the company, who have the right to make a decision on a question of adjournment, and not of the president who has only the duty of presiding."[21]

We see from the case law that selecting or changing the chair of a shareholders meeting may be contentious.

§ 2 Meeting Rules

Many nonprofit organizations adopt *Robert's Rules* or another recognized parliamentary reference book for their meeting rules. The outside source can be adopted in the organization's bylaws, policies or at the beginning of a business meeting through what is commonly termed a "standing rule." Similarly, under the *Standard Code*, an organization can adopt a reference book on parliamentary procedure.[22]

Many organizations, especially large corporations, create and adopt their own meeting rules.

A common practice of business corporations is not adopting an outside reference. Instead, they may create their own, or a hybrid. This may make it more difficult for the corporation attendees to be familiar with the applicable meeting rules. Moreover—adding to the complexity—procedural rules for meetings are subject to various federal and state laws. Added to the mix are bylaws and organizational policies that have a bearing on how the meeting is run.

When a parliamentary reference *is* adopted, these other sources of meeting rules usually supersede it.

The *Standard Code*, a well-regarded parliamentary reference, notes the importance of applicable legal requirements and their significance when working with a parliamentary authority.[23]

A 1990 New York case, citing an earlier New York case, referred to the importance of common meeting practice in the absence of controlling legal authority:

> [I]t was held in Young v. Jebbett H., 213 A.D. 744 at 779, 211 N.Y.S. 61 (4th Dept. 1925) that "in the absence of express regulations by statute or by-law, the conduct of meetings [and elections] is controlled ... by fundamental usage ... common practice [and] [t]he general rule ... that all who are entitled to take part shall be treated with fairness and good faith."[24]

The adoption of meeting rules is fundamental to most meetings and should never be taken for granted. The predetermined rules give attendees a common frame of reference. Their impact may weigh heavily on what decisions are reached.

ROBERT'S RULES

Courts on occasion are influenced by or cite *Robert's Rules*. However, other courts have rejected their applicability in deciding a case. What is clear is that when there is a legal challenge, parliamentary references such as *Robert's Rules* are preempted by applicable legal authority.

A 1982 Florida federal district court, however, showed deference to *Robert's Rules*. It noted that the shareholders agreed to use *Robert's Rules of Order* to conduct a shareholders' meeting. It appears that the court thought that the procedures in *Robert's Rules* are "fair to the parties."[25] For example, the parties agreed on "equal time for presentations at the meeting, and speakers from the floor will be asked to alternate between 'pro' and 'con' on the resolutions to be presented."[26]

Robert's Rules specifically recommends alternating speakers during debate between those who favor and those who oppose a motion.[27]

MORE ON *ROBERT'S RULES*

Other examples of courts that mention *Robert's Rules* favorably or unfavorably in their written opinions are noted below.

Robert's Rules was cited by a 1966 New York case as authority on the question of whether a shareholders meeting could be adjourned.[28]

Robert's Rules was recognized by the U.S. District Court for the District of Columbia for this proposition: "A member has a right to change his vote [at a shareholders meeting] up to the time the result is announced; after that, he can make the change only by the unanimous consent of the assembly granted without debate."[29]

On the other hand, a 1977 Virginia case illustrates the preeminence of state statutes over *Robert's Rules*. The court decided an issue involving a disappearing quorum at a shareholders meeting based on provisions of Virginia's statutory law and corporate bylaws, not on *Robert's Rules*.[30]

CHAIR'S AUTHORITY ON MAKING RULES

A 2008 Delaware case featured a situation where shareholders meeting attendees agreed to a rule that "the Chairman has the authority to decide all procedural issues regarding the conduct of the meeting including adjournment."[31]

This led to controversy. It was claimed that the chair acted improperly when she was asked by a meeting participant for a vote count.

The chair ruled this request out of order and thus, the court concluded, the Chair "was stalling for time."[32] The court asserted, "If an electoral contestant assumes the role of presiding over a meeting, she has an obligation to do so fairly."[33]

In this writer's opinion, granting the presiding officer blanket authority to decide all procedural issues as they arise should be avoided. The organization is best served by having meeting rules decided in advance of its business meetings. In addition, the meeting ground rules specific to an organization, often called "special rules," should be decided on and documented in advance. This helps protect all parties and insures that procedures are more predictable.

§ 3 Selected Parliamentary Procedures

Business corporation case law makes occasional reference to common parliamentary concepts and procedures that are included in parliamentary references. It must be emphasized that parliamentary references also describe (when applicable to business corporations) many other types of motions and procedures for meetings. They are beyond the scope of this book. A small sample is set out below and elsewhere in this book. Readers are urged to consult *Robert's Rules*, the *Standard Code*, and the other fine references to learn the many other details and use of parliamentary procedure.

NEED FOR A SECOND FOR A MOTION

With some exceptions, a second is needed for motions.[34] However, if obtaining a second is overlooked but the motion is debated and/or a vote begun, lack of a second is deemed a harmless error. It does not affect the validity of any proposal adopted.[35]

A New York case featured an annual meeting that was being held in accordance with *Robert's Rules*.[36] A resolution was offered but the chair refused to put the resolution to a vote, claiming that *Robert's Rules* required a second to hold a vote on a resolution. The court ruled that under *Robert's Rules* no second is required in a small board or a committee.[37] "The purpose of a 'Second' is to prevent time from being wasted on motions that have no possibility of passage."[38]

While it is good practice to always require a second, there are situations when a second is not needed. For example, nominations for office do not require a second (unless there is a rule otherwise).

RESCIND

Rescission is essentially the erasure of a motion that has been previously adopted. Normally, a motion for rescission is voted on at a meeting to undo a proposition approved at an earlier meeting. To avoid confusion, specific reference to the rolled-back motion should be made at the meeting where it is rescinded.Parliamentary references[39] impose no time limit on making a rescission motion. For example, it could be a year or two later. The motion may be made by any member, regardless of how he or she first voted on the original motion.

A 2015 federal case in Missouri concerned a factual dispute that arose regarding whether rescission of a resolution was voted on at a board meeting.[40] The minutes of the previous meeting were referred to in order to try to figure it out.[41] A 1996 Louisiana case involved shareholders who voted to rescind approval of a stock exchange.[42]

A cousin of the motion to rescind is the motion to reconsider. The latter is used when an action affirmatively decided upon at a meeting is re-voted on later in the same meeting or in the same session. The mechanism to do so is initiated by a motion to reconsider.

OUT OF ORDER

"Out of order" is a ruling by a presiding officer either that a member is acting inappropriately or his or her comments are inappropriate. It is also a term and device used when a meeting procedure is in error or out of place[43] or for other claimed meeting irregularities.

The chair's ruling at a meeting that a director's or shareholder's motion is out of order is assertible in many contexts. It underscores the importance of the presiding officer understanding and correctly applying the organization's bylaws, policies, and meeting procedures. Such a ruling by the chair should not abuse his or her authority or discretion and the decision should be well intentioned, logical, and well supported.

The following are some motions discussed in case law that a chair found were out of order:

- for a chair to be removed;[44]
- for an election of a new chair;[45]
- for polls to be closed during an election of officers;[46] and
- for a declaration that two formal proxies at a shareholder's meeting were invalid.[47]

POINT OF ORDER

A point of order may be raised when a participant or the chair contends that a meeting rule or procedure was violated. Under *Robert's Rules*, the presiding officer decides all points of order.[48]

A Pennsylvania case mentions this declaration being used by a presiding officer. The circumstances related to shareholder nominations for directors. It was alleged that the nominations failed to comply with a provision in a bank's bylaws.[49]

Under traditional parliamentary references, a meeting member may raise a point of order and the chair must rule on it. Because of its potential importance, the member raising the point of order does not have to first be recognized by the chair; he or she may interrupt another speaker.

Under *Robert's Rules*, a chair's ruling is appealable. The appeal seeking to overrule the chair is decided by all attendees. Reversing the chair's ruling takes a two-thirds vote. The principle explaining this possible appeal from the decision of the chair is that a meeting is run by the chair but "owned" by the collective attendees.

---

1 American Institute of Parliamentarians, Standard Code of Parliamentary Procedure 271 (2012) [hereinafter Standard Code].

2 Artmann v. Ctr. Garage, Inc., 2012 WL 5183577, at *4 (N.D. Ind. Oct. 18, 2012). The bylaw stated that "[t]he president shall preside at all meetings of shareholders and directors."

3 Wheeler v. United States, 2015 WL 5675763, at *2 (E.D. Ky. Sept. 28, 2015).

4 Standard Code, *supra* note 1, at 175.

5 Henry M. Robert III, Daniel H. Honemann, Thomas J. Balch, Daniel E. Seabold & Shmuel Gerber, Robert's Rules of Order Newly Revised §41. (12th ed. 2020) [hereinafter Robert's Rules]. An agenda may be customarily adopted by a majority vote. After the agenda has been adopted, changes can only be made by a two-thirds vote, a vote of the majority of the entire membership, or by unanimous consent.

6 Findings of Fact and Conclusions of Law, Butler v. Moore, 2015 WL 1409676, at *25 (D. Mass. Mar. 26, 2015) (No. 10-10207-FDS) ("At a minimum, however, the fact that the subject was on the agenda indicates that the issue had not been finalized.")

7 ITC Cellular, Inc. v. Morris, 909 S.W.2d 182, 184 (Tex. App. 1995).

8 *Id.*

9 Auerbach Acquisition Assocs., Inc. v. Daily, No. B186116, 2007 WL 2842396 (Cal. Ct. App. Oct. 2, 2007).

10 *Id.*

11 Jordan v. Allegany Co-op Ins. Co., 558 N.Y.S.2d 806, 807 (N.Y.S.2d 1990) ("Since petitioner raises no issue of fraud, self dealing or bad faith concern-

ing the designation of Wilson Gilbert by the Board of Directors, this court holds such designation valid and binding.").

12   Ulloa v. Ulloa (*In re* Annual Meeting of Stockholders of Chamorro Equities, Inc.), No. CVA11-020, 2012 WL 3450308, at 10, 13 (Guam 2012).

13   Kleinberg v. Aharon, No. 12719-VCL, 2017 WL 568342, at *14–15 (Del. Ch. Feb. 13, 2017). The court gave the custodian the following powers:

- The custodian shall have the power to call and set the date and time for meetings of the board.

- The custodian shall preside over any board meeting at which the custodian is present.

- As the presiding officer for the purposes of the meeting, the custodian shall set the agenda for the meeting and oversee the discussion. The custodian may set time limits for discussion and will determine whether to call for a vote.

- A quorum shall exist for a meeting of the board if the custodian and at least three directors are present.

14   Robert's Rules, *supra* note 5, at 62.10.

15   ITC Cellular, Inc. v. Morris, 909 S.W.2d 182, 185. *See also id.* ("There, the Court found that the President defaulted by failing to take charge of the meeting." (citing Duffy v. Loft, 17 Del. Ch. 376, 152 A. 849 (1930))).

16   Capobianco v. First Nat'l Bank of Palmerton, 380 F. Supp. 155 (M.D. Pa. 1974).

17   *Id.* at 162.

18   *In re* Dollinger Corp., 274 N.Y.S.2d 285 (N.Y. Sup. Ct. 1966). The court went on to say: "A quorum was present and if the wishes of the shareholders could be thwarted by the conduct of a single person it would violate all rules of fair play." *Id.* at 288. The court cited *Robert's Rules* § 64, at 259, for the proposition that when at a shareholders meeting certain business must be conducted, an adjourned meeting should fix a new time for the next meeting. *Id.* at 287.

19   *Id.* at 286.

20   *Id.* at 288.

21   *Id.* at. 287. *See also* 18 Guam Code Ann. § 2210 (2020) ("Whenever, from any cause, there is no person authorized to call a meeting, or when the officer authorized to do so refuses, fails or neglects to call a meeting, the judge of the Superior Court on the showing of good cause thereof, may issue an order to any shareholder or member of the corporation...; and if there be no person calling the meeting to preside at such meeting, the judge of the Superior Court may direct the person calling the meeting to preside at the same until a majority of the members of stockholders a majority of the stock present and permitted by law to be voted have chosen one of their number to act as presiding officer for the purpose of the meeting.").

22 Standard Code, *supra* note 1, at 246.

23 "Great care should be given to the selection of a parliamentary authority because the courts do not excuse any organization from its legal requirements because of errors, omissions, or ambiguities in the authority which may have been adopted. Ignorance of the correct rules of procedure is not a valid defense against legal entanglements or action." Standard Code, *supra* note 1, at 246. (citing *In re* Koliba, 338 B.R. 48, 50 (Bankr. N.D. Ohio 2006)). *See also* Robert's Rules, *supra* note 5, at 486

("A board . . . can adopt its own rules, provided that they do not conflict with anything in the legal instrument under which the board is constituted.").

24 Jordan v. Allegany Co-op Ins. Co., 558 N.Y.S.2d 806, 807 (N.Y. 1990).

25 C.A. Cavendes, Sociedad Financiera v. Fla. Nat'l Banks of Fla., Inc., 556 F. Supp. 254, 256 (M.D. Fla. 1982).

26 *Id.*

27 Robert's Rules, *supra* note 5 §§ 3.33(3), 42:9(3). For a lengthy and excellent description of the proper rules of debate, see *id.* §43:1-40 and elsewhere. A summary of that discussion is beyond the scope of this book.

28 *In re* Dollinger Corp., 274 N.Y.S.2d 285, 287 (N.Y. Sup. Ct. 1966) ("Robert's Rules of Order is a recognized authority on parliamentary procedure and in § 64, page 259 it is stated: 'In the case of an annual meeting, where certain business for the year, as the election of officers, must be attended to during the session, the Meeting should fix a time for an adjourned meeting and then adjourn.'").

29 Bender v. Jordan, 439 F. Supp. 2d 139, 174 (D.D.C. 2006) (quoting Robert's Rules § 45, at 395). The court went on to say, "That language contemplates the result being announced at the same meeting, giving each voting member an equal opportunity to change his vote should he so desire; if this provision has effect after the meeting has adjourned, then the latter clause is deprived of meaning." *Id.*

30 Levisa Oil Corp. v. Quigley, 234 S.E.2d 257 (Va. 1977). Yet the court refers approvingly to *Robert's Rules. Id.* at 261 ("It appears that parliamentary procedure accords with the Textron, Inc. approach." (citing Henry M. Robert et al., Robert's Rules of Order Newly Revised § 39, at 296–97 (7th ed. 1970)).

31 Portnoy v. Cry-Cell, Int'l, Inc., 940 A.2d 43 (Del. Ch. 2008). *See also In re* Ebix, Inc., 2016 WL 208402, at *7 (Del. Ch. Jan. 15, 2016) (stating that a corporation had a "control of meeting bylaw [which] gives a meeting chairman—either the Chairman of the Board or the Board's designee—discretion and authority over how the meeting is run").

32 *Portnoy*, 940 A.2d at 62.

33 *Id.* at 79.

34 Under Robert's Rules, motions not needing a second include motions for in-

dividual nominations for office, motions filling in the blanks of a motion on the floor, and motions in small meetings involving twelve or fewer people.

35   Robert's Rules, *supra* note 5 § 4:13.

36   SSM Realty Grp., LLC v. 20 Sherman Assocs., LLC, No. 108147/2010, slip op. 33389 (N.Y. Sup. Ct. Mar. 2, 2012).

37   *Id.*

38   *Id.* at 3. The court noted the plaintiff's argument that a second is not needed "where . . . the chair 'is certain that a motion meets with wide approval, but members are slow in seconding it.'" (citing an unidentified passage of *Robert's Rules*).

The lack of a second was mentioned in Giulietti v. Giulietti, 784 A.2d 905, 951 n.42 (Conn. App. Ct. 2001): "Because attorney Giulietti refused to second the motion, however, it was not even voted on, and Joanne was not reinstated."

39   Robert's Rules, *supra* note 5 § 35:3.

40   Chavis Van & Storage of Myrtle Beach, Inc. v. United Van Lines, LLC, 784 F.3d 1183 (8th Cir. 2015).

41   *Id.* at 1192–93. The corporation claimed that this motion was made at a board meeting and cited the minutes:

"Notwithstanding the adoption of such proposal, it was later rescinded by the Board by a vote of seventeen to one. In connection with the rescission, the Board instructed the Operations Committee to consider the matter . . . ." *Id.* at 1192.

42   Olinde v. 400 Group, 686 So. 2d 883 (La. Ct. App. 1996). The reported vote was 55.6% of the shareholders in favor and 44.4% against. *Id.* at 898.

43   For example, Levisa Oil Corp. v. Quigley, 234 S.E.2d 257 (Va. 1977), featured two motions being ruled out of order by the chair at a shareholders meeting.

44   Biolase, Inc. v. Oracle Partners, L.P., 97 A.3d 1029 (Del. 2014).

45   *In re* Comscape Telecomms., Inc., 423 B.R. 816 (Bankr. S.D. Ohio 2010).

46   Portnoy v. Cryo-Cell Int'l, Inc., 940 A.2d 43, 61 (Del. Ch. 2008).

47   Bender v. Jordan, 439 F. Supp. 2d 139, 136 (D.D.C. 2006).

48   Robert's Rules, *supra* note 5 § 47:7. However, the presiding officer's ruling may be appealed to the rest of the assembly.

49   Capobianco v. First Nat'l Bank of Palmerton, 380 F. Supp. 155 (M.D. Pa. 1974). The court disagreed and found that the nominations were not out of order.

CHAPTER 2

Ex-officio Meeting Positions

§ 4 General Discussion

An ex-officio member of a board or committee automatically holds that position because of another position he or she holds. Ex-officio positions are created by the organization's governing document, but they may be precluded by law or other factors. Ex-officio status on a board can be held by virtue of another position within the same organization or in another organization.

Under *Robert's Rules*, an organization's president is often an ex-officio member of all committees (except the nominating committee and perhaps the disciplinary committee) under organizations' bylaws.[1]

Case law reveals few or no procedural disputes or lawsuits regarding ex-officio status in business corporations. Typically, the chair of the board or the president, or both, are ex-officio members of certain committees, such as the compensation committee. Other officials of the corporation may also be named in the corporate documents as ex-officio committee members.

It is recommended that the bylaws specifically define the role and standing of an ex-officio member rather than taking anything for granted. For example, it should be stated in the corporate documents whether the ex-officio member's presence or lack of presence at a meeting is counted in the quorum determination.

Additionally, the bylaws should specify whether an ex-officio member of a board or committee is entitled to vote. (This detail is often overlooked when bylaws are drafted.)

Corporation case law implies that absent documents stating otherwise, ex-officio members have full participation and voting rights at meetings.

The parliamentary references do not address whether an ex-officio member who may not vote also may not propose a motion. In this writer's opinion, the better view is that when ex-officio members can not vote, they can not offer a motion. However, they may (and are expected to) participate in debate.

The parliamentary references differ on whether ex-officio directors are counted in the quorum determination.[2] Counting them in business corporations seems to be assumed in case law.

CASE LAW EXAMPLES

In a Delaware case, the president of an association was noted to be an ex officio member of a national council.[3] In a Louisiana case, it was mentioned that the president of a bank was an ex-officio member of a review committee.[4] A California case featured a director of human resources who was an ex-officio member of a compensation committee.[5]

In an Alabama federal case, the court wrote that a chief executive officer "was an ex-officio member of the . . . Executive and Credentials Committee, which has among its responsibilities the periodic review of the performance and clinical competence of staff members."[6] And in a 2019 Texas case, it was noted that a Lead Independent Director was an ex-officio member of an Audit Committee.[7]

1   Henry M. Robert III, Daniel H. Honemann, Thomas J. Balch, Daniel E. Seabold & Shmuel Gerber Robert's Rules of Order Newly Revised §47.20 (12th ed. 2020) [hereinafter Robert's Rules].

     Moreover, under *Robert's Rules*, an ex-officio member of a committee has the same rights as any other member but is not obligated to attend and is not counted in the quorum. The *Standard Code*, however, states that an ex-officio member *is* counted in determining a quorum in a committee. AMERICAN INSTITUTE OF PARLIAMENTARIANS, STANDARD CODE OF PARLIAMENTARY PROCEDURE 271 (2012) [hereinafter STANDARD CODE]. *See* Marshall v. Planz, 145 S. Supp. 2d 1258 n.29 (M.D. Ala. 2001).

2   Under the *Standard Code*, an ex-officio member of a committee is counted in determining a quorum and has all of the rights of a member. Standard Code, *supra* note 1, at 190. In contrast, under *Robert's Rules*, the president, when an ex-officio member of a committee is not counted in determining if a quorum is present or in determining what the quorum requirement is. Robert's Rules, *supra* note 1, at 497.

3   KFC Nat'l Council & Advert. Coop. v. KFC Corp., 2011 WL 350415, at *8–9 (Del. Ch. Jan. 31, 2011) (involving a nonprofit organization).

4   Jenson v. First Guar. Bank, 699 So. 2d 403, 407 (La. Ct. App. 1997). *See also* Ash v. Brunswick Corp., 405 F. Supp. 234, 243 (D. Del. 1975) (mentioning the chairman of the board as an ex-officio member of all committees, including a committee appointed to administer a plan); *In re* Walt Disney Co., Consol., 2004 WL 2050138, at *14 (Del. Ch. Sept. 10, 2004) (noting that the president of a company was an ex-officio member of the Compensation Committee but that he "abstained" from attending a "meeting where a substantial part of his own compensation was to be discussed and decided upon").

5   Buster v. Comp. Comm. of the Bd. of Dirs. of Mechanics Bank (N.D. Cal. 2017).

6   Marshall, 145 F. Supp. 2d 1258 n.29.

7   Plaisance v. Schiller, 2019 WL 1205628, at p.7 (S.D. Tex. Mar. 14, 2019). As an ex officio member, the director was allegedly "closely linked" to the company's financial statements.

CHAPTER 3

Executive Session

§ 5 Description

Virtually all leading parliamentary references allow for the holding of an executive session for nonprofit organizations, especially for some parts of or all of board meetings. Committee meetings may and sometimes should be held in an executive session. An executive session takes place when a meeting is held in secret. Both discussions in and results of the meeting are held in strictest confidence. However, some or all results (but not discussions) may be publicly reported if the board or committee decides to do so. The meeting minutes are kept confidential.

As described in parliamentary references, entering into an executive session requires an internal rule, established custom, or motion. Any such motion must be passed by a majority vote. Only board or committee members may attend a board or committee meeting, as the case may be, unless someone is specifically invited by a majority of the other attendees or people entitled to attend.[1]

Sensitive topics may unexpectedly come up during open meetings that call for changing to executive session. The chair or an attendee may sense the need to interrupt an open meeting due to a sensitive subject. In such an event, a motion should be made (and passed by a majority vote) to go into an executive session. A motion is also needed to leave an executive session. When applicable, a meeting agenda may already include entering into executive session.

Executive sessions of board meetings take various forms.[2] Parts of a meeting or an entire meeting may be held in an executive session. Specified attendees may be asked to leave and then rejoin a meeting together or one at a time. There should be valid and justifiable reasons to support who is invited and who is excluded. Challenges reported in case law are rare. Most but not all case law that mentions executive sessions is in the nonprofit arena.

Among the principal reasons the case law suggests a corporate board go into an executive session are the following:

- sensitive legal advice from corporate counsel,[3]
- discussion of sensitive strategic matters, and[4]
- personnel matters.

Discussions about intellectual property are also sensitive and may be appropriate for executive session. Whether a sufficient conflict of interest exists to justify the holding of an executive session and thus restricting attendance is a question of fact.[5] The law may also require that certain corporate meetings must be held publicly.

WHO MAY ATTEND

Questions may arise about who may attend. Some examples and considerations follow.

There may be a perceived or actual conflict of interest between management and nonmanagement directors on certain topics. Management directors may be asked not to attend or to leave a board meeting. For example, employment matters may be discussed.[6] Similarly, interests of "independent" directors versus officers of the corporation may require a separate meeting.[7] A 2014 California opinion states, "the independent directors met in executive session to discuss [a director's] options, and the directors' duties to shareholders."[8]

A 2012 Delaware state case mentions that discussion of executive compensation by a compensation committee was done "in executive session," with nonemployee directors of the company present."[9] A Louisiana case discusses an executive session during which a bank president "discussed Management's plans for enhancement of the capital of the Bank."[10]

When an executive session is called for a board meeting, the board must decide who to exclude from the meeting.[11] A 2010 New York case featured a common board meeting held in an executive session that included only "Independent Directors."[12]

COMMITTEES

Committees may and sometimes should go into an executive session[13] for the same reasons and using the same procedures as boards. Their minutes and other meeting materials are also confidential.

---

1   Henry M. Robert III, Daniel H. Honemann, Thomas J. Balch, Daniel E. Seabold & Shmuel Gerber, Robert's Rules of Order Newly Revised (12th ed. 2020) [hereinafter Robert's Rules].

Disciplinary matters and other matters must be held in executive session. The *Standard Code* uses the term "closed meeting." AMERICAN INSTITUTE OF PARLIAMENTARIANS, STANDARD CODE OF PARLIAMENTARY PROCEDURE 271 (2012) [hereinafter STANDARD CODE]. The *Standard Code* also lists as appropriate for executive session personnel matters, legal issues, and other highly sensitive matters that could harm the organization if made public.

2   Of course, the use of executive sessions may be affected by governmental or other requirements.

3   *In re* Tibco Software Inc. Stockholders Litig., No. 10319-CB (Del. Ch. Nov. 25, 2014) (legal advisor present during discussion with Goldman); RBC Capital Mkts., LLC v. Jervis, 129 A.3d 816 n.21 (Del. 2015) (legal counsel discussed with the board a legal holding in another Chancery Court decision); Standard Code, *supra* note 1, at 108 (stating that pending legal matters and other topics which if made public could harm the organization should be held in a closed meeting).

4   *In re* Answers Corp. S'holders Litig., No. 6170-VCN, at n.16 (Del. Ch. Feb.

13, 2014) ("Specifically, the Board considered strategic alternatives during an executive session of its . . . meeting; the Board 'continued to believe it was in the best interests of the Company and its stockholders to explore strategic alternatives such that it would be fully informed' . . . .");

See also Jenson v. First Guar. Bank, 699 So. 2d 403 (La. Ct. App. 1997) (involving an executive session called by a bank president at a board meeting to consider "Management's plans for the enhancement of the capital of the Bank"; the court commented on the executive session minutes).

See also Wilen v. Pamrapo Savings Bank, 429 B.R.152 (Bankr. N.J. 2010) in which an executive session included discussion of extending a repayment date for a line of credit conditioned on a mortgage.

5   Air Products & Chemicals, Inc., 16 A.3d 48, 129 n.61 (Del. Ch. 2011) (finding no conflict of interest in considering an offer was found to justify the holding of an executive session by the independent board members because the stockholders had substantial aligned interests).

    For other case examples in which executive session was used, see Memorandum Opinion, *In re* Anthem-Cigna Mercer Litig., No. 2017-0114-JTL, at 68 (Del. Ch. Aug. 31, 2020), https://law.justia.com/cases/delaware/court-of-chancery/2020/c-a-no-2017-0114-jtl.html (discussing a proposed transaction); Memorandum Opinion, Mehra v. Teller, No. 2019-0812-KSJM, at 36 (Del. Ch. Jan. 29, 2021), https://law.justia.com/cases/delaware/court-of-chancery/2021/c-a-no-2019-0812-ksjm.html.

6   Klaassen v. Allegro Dev. Corp., No. 8626-VCL (Del. Ch. Oct. 11, 2013) (featuring non-management directors and the CEO being asked to leave a meeting so the remaining directors could meet in an executive session to discuss employment matters.

7   *In re* Massey Energy Co. Derivative & Class Action Litig., No. 5430-VCS (Del. Ch. May 31, 2011) (plan for outside directors to have an executive session regarding open market purchases). *See also In re* Dole Food Co., No. 8703-VCL, 2015 WL 5052214, at *28 (Del. Ch. Aug. 27, 2015) (executive session for the outside directors with counsel).

8   Cinotto v. Levine, No. B242191, 2014 WL 4604750, at *7 (Cal. Ct. App. Sept. 16, 2014).

9   Freedman v. Adams, No. 4199-VCN, at n.49 (Del. Ch. Mar. 30, 2012).

10   Jenson v. First Guar. Bank, 699 So.2d 403, 405 (La. Ct. App. 1997).

11   Wilen v. Pamrapo Sav. Bank (In re Bayonne Med. Ctr.), 429 B.R. 152, 168 (Bankr. N.J. 2010) (featuring an executive session of trustees from which guests, including the acting CFO and other staff, were excluded);

    Klaassen v. Allegro Dev. Corp., 106 A.3d 1035, 1041 (Del. 2014) (involving a board that met in an executive session during which the CEO was removed and replaced; the CEO and others were first asked to leave the room).

12   *See, e.g., In re* Reserve Fund Sec. & Derivative Litig., 732 F. Supp. 2d 310

(S.D.N.Y. 2010); *In re* Lear Corp. S'holders Litig., 926 A.2d 94, 104 (Del. Ch. 2007).

A 2018 case out of the U.S. District Court for the Southern District of Indiana featured independent outside directors who held an executive session without company directors. "At the executive sessions, directors discussed concerns and developed recommendations for management." Levin v. Miller, 900 F.3d 856, 858 (7th Cir. 2018).

13   *See, e.g., In re* Investors Bancorp. Inc., C.A. No. 12327-VCS, 2017 WL 1277672, at *5 (Del. Ch. Apr. 5, 2017) (featuring a compensation committee that went into executive session from which the company's president and COO were excluded).

CHAPTER 4

Minutes of Meetings

§ 6 Significance

Minutes taken at a meeting are a significant legal document—especially in the context of litigation. Under *Robert's Rules*, "the minutes should contain mainly a record of what was *done* at the meeting, not what was *said* by the members. The minutes should never reflect the secretary's opinion, favorable or otherwise, on anything said or done."[1] Other pertinent information may and sometimes should be included. For example, certain notices of future action, such as proposed bylaw amendments, pertinent committee reports, and future meeting dates should be included. In this writer's opinion, there is a tendency to include too much inappropriate information. Meeting minutes are not meant to be used as a transcript of everything that was said.

Meeting minutes are a business record and subject to all statutory and evidentiary rules governing their availability and use as evidence. State corporation statutes record them to be taken as a spontaneous record of what took place—whether they are called "minutes" or some other term.

Their reliability, accuracy, and completeness are open to challenge in litigation.

Committees should also take accurate minutes of their meetings. For example, a special meeting of an audit committee kept minutes.[2]

§ 7 Unintended Uses

Sometimes minutes are used in unexpected ways. Therefore, the procedures used for taking minutes can have unintended legal consequences. This should be considered in advance of a meeting. Here are some examples:

- Minutes may be used as a writing to satisfy a requirement that some other document, such as a contract, must be in writing—especially if the minutes are signed by a corporate officer.
- Minutes may be interpreted as a legal document that must be signed. For example, when all shareholders sign them, minutes may be used as evidence that they (the shareholders) approved a transaction.
- The existence of minutes may constitute evidence of corporate authority.

EXAMPLES OF THEIR IMPACT

The following is a sample of the numerous published cases that demonstrate the wide-ranging and sometimes unexpected legal effect of meeting minutes.

A 2017 New Mexico case featured a motion that was offered for a "Determination of the Effect of Minutes of the Annual and Special Meeting of Shareholders."[3] The minutes were used to attempt to demonstrate, among other actions, the removal of certain directors, officers, and employees and the election of some directors and the president, vice president, secretary, and treasurer at a meeting.

In a 2014 West Virginia case, the facts involved meeting minutes that were signed by all shareholders. As a result, the court concluded, "The minutes of the . . . board meeting constitute a signed writing sufficient to modify the Redemption Agreement."[4]

Minutes were used as the best evidence to establish corporate authority in a 2008 Ohio case.[5] The trial court stated, "There are a number of ways that corporate authority can be established. The minutes of a corporation are the best evidence of authority . . . ."[6]

A 2013 California case[7] involved corporate bylaws that provided that approval of minutes may be used to verify that a meeting is valid, including how it was called and how notice of it was given. Another example is a 2014 Delaware Chancery Court opinion that featured meeting minutes being used as an exhibit in a claim of fraud.[8] And a 2012 New York case involved meeting minutes that were used to note attendance at meetings and discussions that took place.[9]

Attendance at a meeting, as reflected by corporate minutes, was used to establish that an attendee knew certain facts.[10]

In a 1997 Louisiana decision, the court noted that board minutes showed that a recapitalization "plan and other proposals were being considered, but none had been chosen as an exclusive plan." It was noted that a contract was not formed.[11]

Another example of a court using meeting minutes as evidence of what happened at a board meeting is a 2001 Delaware Chancery Court opinion.[12] Approval of minutes supported "defendants' contention that the board did make [a party] a record date-setting committee. Important to this decision is the board's June 1, 2001 approval of minutes for the April 1, 2001 meeting that formally reflect a resolution to this effect."[13]

Board meeting minutes involved in a Maryland case were reviewed by a Special Litigation Committee as a part of its investigation.[14]

In sum, meeting minutes should not be taken for granted. Properly prepared and used, they have the potential to defend an organization against challenges. Otherwise, the minutes could cause unintended legal exposure for an organization.

§ 8 Failure to Take

Taking and maintaining proper corporate meeting minutes is essential. Applicable state law should be consulted. For example, the court in an Illinois federal case applying state law in 2008 noted that "failure to maintain records of meeting minutes is proof that it [the corporation] failed to adhere to the corporate form."[15]

When minutes are not taken, suspicions about why they were not taken can arise. Not taking them at all may be a factor in a court allowing a party to "pierce the corporate veil" in its search for a deep pocket, as occurred in the Illinois case mentioned in the previous paragraph. Conflicting memories and confusion about what took place at a meeting further complicate matters.

The authority of the board is reflected and executed by decisions explicitly set forth in the minutes.

§ 9 Draft Minutes

The proper circulation of draft minutes before the next meeting should not be taken for granted. For example, identifying who receives the drafts between meetings should not be left to chance. The confusion and problems that can arise from the circulating of "draft minutes" are demonstrated in a 2016 Delaware case.[16]

Business corporations should consider adopting formal policies about who receives a copy of draft minutes and at what time. Similarly, what changes, if any, may be made to these minutes in advance of the next meeting should not be left to chance.

§ 10 Reports to the Board

The scope of the statutory right of shareholders to inspect minutes is discussed in a 2014 Alaska case.[17] A shareholder sought not only the board minutes but also all the meeting presentations and reports. In rejecting the shareholder's request, the court stated,

"We therefore hold that the statutory category "MINUTES" does not ordinarily encompass presentations or reports made to the board but rather merely requires a record of the subjects discussed and actions taken at the meeting, which must be faithfully recorded."[18]

Other courts may take a different view.

§ 11 Approval

Normally, board minutes are reviewed at the next regular meeting and approved by a majority vote. Any participant may request a correction. If a requested change is disputed, a majority vote is required.

Acrimony among board members was reflected in a 2005 Washington case.[19] There was a deadlock over the approval of minutes. "The fight became so bitter that they could not agree on board meeting minutes."[20]

The final wording and content of meeting minutes could have legal and other significance and should not be taken for granted. Members should not be reluctant to request corrections at the next meeting or even later.

§ 12 Secrecy of an Executive Session

Under the *Standard Code*, minutes from an executive session meeting are to be kept separate from those of other meetings. Their security must be maintained. Minutes from a closed session are approved only in another closed session.[21] Some decisions and actions may be deemed to not be secret and the secrecy of some or all portions of the executive session meeting may be lifted by the assembly.[22] This must, of course, be done with caution.

---

1   Henry M. Robert III, Daniel H. Honemann, Thomas J. Balch, Daniel E. Seabold & Shmuel Gerber, Robert's Rules of Order Newly Revised § 48:2 (12th ed. 2020) [hereinafter Robert's Rules]. For a full discussion of minutes, see *id.* at 4811–27.

2   Exec. Risk Indem. v. AFC Enters., Inc., 510 F. Supp. 2d 1308, 1316 (N.D. Ga. 2007).

3   *In re* Sandia Tobacco Mfrs., Inc., 571 B.R. 449 (Bankr. N.M. 2017).

4   Addington v. Raleigh Mine & Indus. Supply, Inc., 2014 WL 3548934 at *27–28 (S.D. W. Va. July 17, 2014).

5   First Nat'l. Bank of Sw. Ohio v. Individual Bus. Servs., Inc., 2008 Ohio 3857 at *12 (Ohio Ct. App. 2008).

6   *Id.*

7   CalPOP.com, Inc. v. Hoover, No. B252595 (Cal. Ct. App. Sept. 3, 2015).

8   Vichi v. Koninklijke Philips Elecs., 85 A.3d 725 (Del. Ch. 2014).

9   Suffolk Anesthesiology Assocs., P.C. v. Verdone, 951 N.Y.S.2d 83 (N.Y. Sup. Ct. 2012).

10 Brumley v. Leam Invs., Inc., No. 09-1078, at 24 (W.D. La. Feb. 16, 2012) ("[The director's] attendance at that meeting and approval of the minutes of that meeting establishes that, on that date, [the director] knew of the existence of the facts which should at least have put [the director] on inquiry. [The director] failed to file suit within two years of that date.").

11 Jenson v. First Guar. Bank, 699 So. 2d 403, 405–06 (La. Ct. App. 1997). Moreover, the court stated: "From our review of board minutes, including the meeting of August 8, as well as meetings before and after, we find that the term 'management' was used repetitively, and unmistakably, in board and executive session minutes to refer to the Bank. Hence, the August 8 highlighted minutes provide no support for a contract between two independent parties."

12 *In re* Staples, Inc. S'holders Litig., 792 A.2d 934, 963 (Del. Ch. 2001). In *Gross v. GFI Group, Inc.*, 310 F. Supp. 3d 384, 389 (S.D.N.Y. 2018), the court used a detailed chronology of numerous meeting minutes from both special and committee and board meetings to provide important background information.

13   *In re* Staples, Inc. S'holders Litig., 792 A.2d at 963.

14   Boland v. Boland, 5 A.3d 106, 130 (Md. Ct. Spec. App. 2010).

15   Wachovia Sec., LLC v. Jahelka, 586 F. Supp. 2d 972, 998 (N.D. Ill. 2008).

16   Memorandum Opinion and Order, Chammas v. Navlink, Inc., No. 11265, at 26–27 (Del. Ch. Feb. 1, 2016). One of the issues was who was entitled to see the draft minutes and challenge their accuracy and validity. "Mere communications among directors regarding draft meeting minutes, where Plaintiffs have not alleged that such communications amount to official corporate business or otherwise affect the corporation's rights or obligations, fall outside the scope of the company's books and records." *Id.* at 27.

17   Pederson v. Arctic Slope Reg'l Corp., 331 P.3d 384 (Alaska 2014).

18   *Id.* at 399. The court cited Alaska Statute 10.06.430(a), which "requires a corporation to keep 'correct and complete . . . minutes of proceedings of its shareholders, board, and committee of the board.' Alaska Statute 10.06.430(b) conveys to shareholders the right to inspect those minutes under the same conditions as it grants the right to inspect 'books and records of account.'" *Id.*

19   Skarbo v. Skarbo Scandinavian Furniture Import, Inc., No. 54288-5-I (Wash. Ct. App. Aug. 15, 2005).

20   *Id.* at 3.

21   American Institute of Parliamentarians, Standard Code of Parliamentary Procedure 228–29 (2012) [hereinafter Standard Code].

22   Robert's Rules, *supra* note 1 § 9:26.

CHAPTER 5

Quorums - Board and Shareholder

§ 13 Quorums for Board Meetings

Without a quorum at a board meeting, official actions requiring a vote are invalid. According to parliamentary references,[1] a quorum is determined on the basis of the number of members present, not how many voted.

The general rule is that the presence at a board meeting of a majority of the total number of directors is necessary to constitute a quorum. If there is a quorum, a board may adopt a measure. Usually, the corporate documents may change the quorum requirements – up to a point. Applicable statutes and corporate documents must be consulted to see their impact on how to define a recognized and acceptable quorum.

This principle is well stated in a Delaware statute: "A majority of the total number of directors shall constitute a quorum for the transaction of business unless the certificate of incorporation or the bylaws require a greater number."[2]

EXCEPTIONS

There are some exceptions to the rule requiring a quorum. There may be extenuating circumstances that require a finding that a proper meeting was held despite the lack of a quorum. For example, when the number of board members holding office is drastically reduced, the remaining board members may be able to act even without a quorum. Applicable law must be determined.

The exception noted above may occur when there are vacancies on the board. Generally, the remaining directors may fill the vacancies by vote even if there is no quorum at the time of the vote. For example, in a 2015 New York case, the court cited a corporate bylaw that stated, "Unless otherwise provided in the Articles of Incorporation or in the bylaws, vacancies and newly-created directorships resulting from any increase in the authorized number of directors may be filled by a majority of the directors then in office, although less than a quorum, or by the sole remaining director."[3]

The principle involved here is that a majority of the directors may fill a vacancy created by an increase in the size of the number of seats, even if less than a quorum is voting.[4] One caution is that the certificate of incorporation or the organization's bylaws may override the state statute.[5]

Consistent with this idea is a 2012 New York case involving a party who commented that "under [New York] BCL 705 (a), a vacancy on the board of directors may be filled with less than a quorum in attendance at a meeting . . . ."[6]

Similarly, a 1987 Alabama case upheld the transaction of business even though the number of directors fell below the minimum required by corporate bylaws. The Alabama court found this permissible so long as the number of directors who vote does not fall below a quorum.[7]

WHO IS COUNTED WHEN CONFLICTS ARISE

An important principle, noted in *Robert's Rules*, is that directors with a conflict of interest are counted in the quorum determination even though they are not permitted to vote. For example, in the Delaware Code it is stated: "Common or interested directors may be counted in determining the presence of a quorum at a meeting of the board of directors or of a committee which authorizes the contract or transaction."[8]

This principle also found support in a 2007 Delaware case, in which the court held that "[u]nder 8 *Del. C.* § 144, a related-party transaction may not be set aside merely due to its self-interested nature if it (a) has been approved by a majority of the disinterested directors of the corporation, even if that majority is not a quorum, (b) has been approved by a majority of the disinterested shareholders, or (c) is fair to the corporation . . . ."[9]

In an interesting 2011 Connecticut case concerning two "sub-units" of a board, the court wrote that "the "board may terminate derivative litigation by a majority vote of . . . the independent directors if they constitute a quorum or . . . a committee composed of at least two independent directors."[10]

We see, then, that a quorum may at times be less than a majority or other designated number when certain attendees are disqualified because of a conflict.

TRICKERY

Courts have held that quorums obtained by trickery, fraud, or duress are invalid.[11] Similarly, preventing directors from attending a meeting is invalid.[12] However, it has been ruled that if the fooled director remains at the entire meeting and participates, he or she has lost the right to object to his or her attendance having been obtained by trickery.[13]

§ 14 Shareholders Meetings

A quorum requirement means that a specified number or percentage of those eligible to vote must attend a meeting for official business to be conducted. Without sufficient attendance, decisions made at a meeting are invalid. The meeting may proceed, but no formal votes may be taken and no formal decisions may be made. For example, committee reports may be offered, but no formal action may be taken on them.

Under a Pennsylvania statute, bylaws may provide for "the number of members that constitute a quorum."[14] This is an area controlled by applicable statutes and common law. The bylaws of the organization should discuss the requirements.

A reported 1982 federal case in Florida featured an unsuccessful motion to adjourn a stockholders meeting for lack of a quorum.[15] The chair rejected the motion, but the court found the chair's ruling to have been in error.

Under *Robert's Rules*, some motions in response to the lack of a quorum are proper; specifically permitted are motions to fix the time to adjourn, adjourn, recess, or take measures to obtain a quorum.[16]

HOW CALCULATED

A majority of the outstanding shares of stock, whether in person or by proxy, usually constitutes a quorum for a shareholders meeting. While there may be exceptions, the denominator is usually based on the total number of outstanding shares, not individual shareholders attending a meeting.

Many statutes provide that a majority of outstanding shares constitutes a quorum. A corporation that wishes to use a different calculation should so specify in its articles of incorporation. Using bylaws to do so is problematic. In any event, defining less than one-third of the outstanding shares of stock as a quorum creates serious procedural problems.

CASE LAW EXAMPLES

Case law offers insights on different ways to calculate the presence of a quorum. A sample of the cases follow.

A 2005 Arkansas case offers an excellent discussion about whether the state statutory provision that a majority of the shares entitled to vote, in person or by proxy, constitutes a quorum is binding.[17] Also discussed in this case is whether the articles of incorporation are the proper and only vehicle for defining a quorum if differently than the statute.

The principle that a majority of outstanding shares of stock constitutes a quorum is enunciated in a 2017 New Mexico case.[18]

A 2004 Arkansas court offered a description taken from a corporation's bylaws:

> A quorum shall be constituted when the person [*sic*] owning at least fifty-one percent (51%) of the outstanding and issued shares of stock, as indicated by the stock transfer register of the corporation, are in attendance. This quorum may transact the business of any meeting of the stockholders of this corporation, and a vote of the majority of such stockholders in attendance at such meeting shall be sufficient to pass or reject any properly proposed measure, except for the transaction of business which requires a different quorum or majority either by statute of this state [Arkansas] or by the Articles of Incorporation of this corporation.[19]

In a 1996 Missouri case, the court, citing a state statute, noted that "a quorum must exist at a corporate shareholders' meeting before business may be legally conducted. A quorum of a meeting of shareholders shall never consist of less than a majority of the outstanding shares entitled to vote."[20]

In an Ohio case, a fifty percent shareholder refused to participate in several shareholder meetings; this resulted in there being no quorum.[21]

In a 1995 Maryland case, the court cited a bank charter and 12 C.F.R. § 5441.1 (1995) for the proposition that "[a]ny number of members present and voting, represented in person or by proxy, at a regular or special meeting of the members shall constitute a quorum. A majority of all votes cast at any meeting of the members shall determine any question."[22]

Under a 2012 Virginia Bankruptcy Court decision, "Unless the charter or bylaws of a corporation provide otherwise, a plurality of all the votes cast at a meeting at which a quorum is present is sufficient to elect a director."[23]

In an interesting 1959 North Carolina case, the court wrote that "stockholders of a corporation may . . . fix more than a majority of shares or members of a corporation for a quorum."[24]

Accordingly, the general rule is that a majority of applicable shares constitutes a quorum for a shareholder meeting unless the proper corporate documents state otherwise and the relevant state statute is not violated.

§ 15 Disappearing Quorum

A vexing problem is the so-called disappearing quorum. This situation occurs when attendees leave after a meeting is convened, causing the loss of a quorum. Sometimes this is done deliberately as a tactic to undermine the legitimacy of a meeting. Case law varies on the subject of disappearing quorums: some jurisdictions allow a meeting to continue and others require that it end. The applicable statute and case law must be reviewed to see which result pertains.[25]

The following is a sample of cases.

In a 1977 Virginia case, it was reported that some shareholders left a meeting but a minority of shareholders remained and proceeded to elect five directors.[26] The trial court "held that the quorum of the annual stockholders meeting of [the company] was lost by the departure of [two stockholders] from the meeting and that, as a consequence, all business conducted thereafter was of no legal effect."[27] The appellate opinion includes an excellent discussion of the subject.

In a 1995 Texas case, the court found differently. The court rejected the contention that a quorum was "broken" when shareholders left a meeting based on a statute, which provides:

> Unless otherwise provided in the articles of incorporation or bylaws, once a quorum is present at a meeting of shareholders, the shareholders represented in person or proxy at the meeting may conduct such business as may be properly brought before the meeting until it is adjourned, and the subsequent withdrawal from the meeting of any shareholder or the refusal of any shareholder represented in person or proxy to vote shall not affect the presence of a quorum at the meeting.[28]

§ 16 Point of Order

Parliamentary references note that a point of order may be made by the chair or a meeting participant to raise a question about the lack of a quorum. This stops voting until the matter is decided. In this writer's opinion, a formal recount should be taken to confirm the presence of a quorum. This should all be reported in the minutes.

In addition, after a recess or when otherwise reconvening, a fresh quorum count is a good idea.

1   American Institute of Parliamentarians, Standard Code of Parliamentary Procedure 123 (2012) [hereinafter Standard Code].

2   8 Del. C. § 141(b) (*cited in* Thermopylae v. Capital Partners, L.P. v. Simbol, Inc., No. 10619-VCG (Del. Ch. Jan. 29, 2016). *See also* Memorandum Opinion, *Sciabacvechi v. Liberty Brandband Corp.*, No. 11428-VCG, at 42 n.211 (Del. Ch. 2018) ("Under 8 *Del. C.* § 141 (b), '[a] majority of the total number of directors shall constitute a quorum for the transaction of business unless the certificate of incorporation or the bylaws require a greater number.' Charter's certificate does not require a greater number, and thus the six directors not appointed by Liberty Broadband constituted a quorum.").

3   Memorandum of Decision & Order, Intelligent Digital Sys., LLC v. Beazley Ins. Co., 12-cv-1209 (ADS)(GRB), at 4 (E.D.N.Y. June 23, 2015), https://law.justia.com/cases/federal/district-courts/new-york/nyed-ce/2:2012cv01209/328150/101/; *accord* Gries Sports Enters., Inc. v. Cleveland Browns Football Co., Inc., 496 N.E.2d. 959, 967 (Ohio 1986) ("The present Delaware Statute provides that a transaction may be approved by a board of directors by the affirmative votes of the majority of the disinterested directors, even though the disinterested directors be less than a quorum. 8 Del. Code Ann. Section 144 (a)(1)."); Church Point Wholesale Beverage Co., Inc. v. Voitier, 706 So.2d. 1015, 1018 (La. Ct. App. 1998).

4   Kurz v. Holbrook, 989 A.2d 140, 155 (Del. Ch. 2010) ("[U]nless otherwise specified in the certificate of incorporation or bylaws, 'newly created directorships resulting from any increase in the authorized number of directors elected by all of the stockholders having the right to vote as a single class may be filled by a majority of the directors then in office, although less than a quorum,'" quoting 8 Del. C. § 223(a)(1)).

5   *See* 15 Pa. Const. Stat. 7721(b) ("Content. --The bylaws may provide . . . the number of members that constitute a quorum.").

6   *In re* Benincaso, 2012 NY Slip Op. 30015 (N.Y. Surr. Ct. Jan. 9, 2012).

7   Adams v. Farlow, 516 So. 2d. 528, 543–44 (Ala. 1987) (quoting the trial court as stating that "[a] Board of Directors may continue to transact the business of the corporation even though the number of directors is reduced below the minimum required by the by-laws provided that the number of directors does not fall below a quorum").

8   8 Del. Code Ann. § 144(b).

9   *In re* Infousa, Inc. S'holders. Litig., 953 A.2d 963, 997 (Del. Ch. 2007).

10 MBIA Inc. v. Fed. Ins. Co., 652 F.3d 152, 163 (2nd Cir. 2011).

11 Klaassen v. Allegro Dev. Corp., No. 8626-VCL (Del. Ch. Nov. 7, 2013).

12 *Id.* at *12 ("Each member of the board has the right to participate in deliberations and consult with his fellow directors, and trickery cannot be permitted to deprive the non-attending director of that right").

13 Dillon v. Berg, 326 F. Supp. 1214, 1221 (D. Del. 1971) (citing 2 Fletcher, Cyclopedia of Corporations § 422 (Perm. Ed. 1969).

14 15 Pa. Const. Stat. §7721(b).

15 C.A. Cavendes, Sociedad Financiera v. Fla. Nat'l Banks, 556 F. Supp. 254, 258 (M.D. Fla. 1982) (finding that the meeting violated the Florida Corporate Code and the corporation's bylaws "by using improper voting procedures (a) to defeat Cavendes' motion to adjourn to a date certain; (b) to determine the outcome of the appeal of the disputed procedure; and (c) to secure adoption of a motion to permanently adjourn *sine die*").

16 Robert's Rules of Order § 40:7.

17 Ray Townsend Farms, Inc. v. Smith, 207 S.W.3d 557, 563 (Ark. App. 2005) ("Our legislature has decreed that a quorum for purposes of a shareholders' meeting is a majority of the shares entitled to vote, unless the corporation's articles of incorporation provide otherwise. . . . The statute permits a deviation from the 'majority of shares' rule only if so provided in the articles of incorporation.").

18 *In re* Sandia Tobacco Mfrs., Inc., 571 B.R. 449, 453 (Bankr. N.M. 2017) ("A majority of shares constitutes a quorum at a shareholders' meeting.").

19 Taylor v. Hinkle, 200 S.W.3d 387, 395 (Ark. 2004).

20 Place v. P.M. Place Stores Co., 950 S.W.2d 862, 866 (Mo. Ct. App. 1996). A significant point raised by this case was the next comment that "the trial court erred in ignoring this legal principle [the need for a quorum] in the name of equity." *Id.*

21 Sapienza v. Material Eng'g & Tech. Support Serv. Corp. (Ohio App. 2011).

22 Ideal Fed. Sav. Bank v. Murphy, 663 A.2d 1272, 1279 (Md. 1995).

23 Matson v. Alpert (*In re* Landamerica Fin. Grp., Inc.), 470 B.R. 759, 789 n.23 (Bankr. E.D. Va. 2012), quoting Md. Code Ann. § 2-404(d).

24 Webb v. Morehead, 111 S.E.2d 586, 590 (N.C. 1959). The court cited the Act of 1955, G.S. 55-65 and 66 (1959 Cum. Supp.). The court further noted, "This power is denied to directors, and cannot be used to prevent the holding of annual meetings." *Id.*

25 For example, the Pennsylvania Business Statute distinguishes between a disappearing quorum at a shareholders meeting and at a board meeting ("Committee comment – 2013. Unlike the case of a shareholders meeting, where, under 15 Pa. C. S. § 1756 (a) (2), the shareholders can continue to do business notwithstanding the withdrawal of enough shareholders to leave less than a quorum, Subsection (a) requires that a quorum be present whenever action is taken by the board of directors. If for example, four matters

are to be considered at a meeting of the board at which a quorum is present at the start of the meeting, but enough directors to destroy the existence of a quorum leave the meeting after two of the matters have been considered, actions properly taken on the first two matters will be valid but the meeting will not be able to act on the last two matters.").

26   Levisa Oil Corp. v. Quigley, 234 S.E.2d 257, 259, 261 (Va. 1977). The court cited Virginia Code § 13.1-31, which stated: "Unless otherwise provided in the articles of incorporation, a majority of the shares entitled to vote, represented in person or by proxy, shall constitute a quorum at a meeting of stockholders. . . . Less than a quorum may adjourn the meeting." Later in the opinion, the court wrote: "When [Stockholder A and Stockholder B] withdrew from the meeting there no longer existed a quorum, and any action thereafter taken by the stockholders, other than to adjourn the meeting to a future time, was void and of no effect.").

27   *Id.*

28   ITC Cellular, Inc. v. Morris, 909 S.W. 2d 182 (Tex. App.1995). *See also* Florie v. Reinhart, 2017 Tex. App. LEXIS 1798, at *24–25, 29 (Tex. App. 2017). However, the trial court found that the departing shareholder was "misled . . . into believing the meeting was over, despite the lack of a formal vote on adjournment."

CHAPTER 6

Board Meetings

§ 17 Electronic Means

Under most if not all state business corporation statutes, boards may meet by telephone.[1] This practice has become commonplace. The organization's bylaws should also address the subject.

Under *Robert's Rules*, an electronic meeting "does not lose its character as a deliberative assembly . . . so long as the meetings provide, at a minimum, conditions of opportunity for simultaneous [oral] communication among all participating members equivalent to those of meetings held in one room or area."[2]

While at times a bit awkward, the same rules of procedure used for in-person meetings should be used for electronic meetings. For example, the same rules apply as to who may speak in debate and for how long.

§ 18 Unanimous Consent

Certain action may be taken by a board without a meeting if there is unanimous consent. Unanimous consent should be put in writing. For example, a 2004 Tennessee federal case quoted a state statute that provided as follows:

Unless the charter or bylaws provide otherwise, action required or permitted [under the Tennessee statute] to be taken at a board of directors meeting may be taken without a meeting. If all directors consent to taking such action without a meeting, the affirmative vote of the number of directors that would be necessary to authorize or take such action at a meeting is the act of the board. The action must be evidenced by one (1) or more written consents describing the action taken, signed by each director in one (1) or more counterparts, indicating each signing director's vote or abstention on the action, and shall be included in the minutes or filed with the corporate records reflecting the action taken.[3]

In the strictest parliamentary sense, unanimous consent takes place at a meeting when all parties agree to adopt a motion and waive their opportunity to first debate the measure. Groups of noncontroversial motions may be decided with one vote unless there is an objection by an attendee to a particular motion. If there is an objection, then the specific motion must be offered, debated, and then voted on.

OTHER MEETING DETAILS

State business statutes cover most, if not all, of the usual meeting details. However, when permissible, the organization's bylaws may also cover some or all of these topics. This includes, for example, details about the notice and location of the meeting.

§ 19 Proxies

Directors are not permitted to use proxies at board meetings in either for-profit or nonprofit organizations.[4] It is believed that the director's personal expertise and insight is lost when he or she is not in attendance to vote.

§ 20 Waiver of Notice

Waiver of a meeting notice by an attendee is recognized by the law.

For example, a court in New Mexico noted that "[a]ttendance of a director at a meeting of the board constitutes waiver of notice of the meeting unless the director attends for the express purpose of contesting the authority of the board to act."[5]

Applicable statutes and case law should be consulted regarding how an effective objection to faulty notice may be made. As mentioned, mere attendance may constitute a waiver of a faulty notice if the notice is not properly objected to at the meeting. The objection should be made at the beginning of the meeting.

If a director attends a meeting believing there was faulty notice, that director should attempt and arguably has the right to have that contention included in the meeting minutes. Any applicable state statute should be consulted.

§ 21 Notice of Special Meetings

Notices of special board meetings, by their nature, require care in their timing, delivery, and content. Every business corporation must determine and follow the law that applies to it and its own individual corporate requirements. Failure to do so can lead to a challenge to the validity of the meeting and its results.

Under *Robert's Rules*, "[n]otice of the time, place, and purpose of the meeting, clearly and specifically describing the subject matter of the motions or items of business to be brought up, must be sent to all members a reasonable number of days in advance."[6]

Notice of a special board meeting must comply with state statutory requirements and the organization's governing documents. Typically, three or more days' notice or more is required. The subjects to be discussed and considered must be specifically stated in the notice. Every director must receive the notice.

The notice must be proper. For example, a court in Delaware found in 2015 that a notice of a special board meeting was defective because it did not contain an agenda of the topics to be covered at the meeting.[7]

In a 1996 Virgin Islands case, the court ruled that a notice for a special meeting "shall contain a statement of the business to be transacted thereat, and that no business other than that specified in the call for the meeting shall be transacted at any such meeting."[8]

If a director attends the special meeting and does not object to his or her notice at the beginning of the meeting, he or she has waived any notice deficiency.[9] State statutes and case law describe in detail how this objection must be made to be effective. In this writer's opinion, the objector should also request at the time of the meeting that his or her objection be included in the meeting minutes.

SIGNIFICANT TRANSACTIONS

Certain proposed actions at a board meeting may trigger heightened notice requirements common to special meetings. These are sometimes called "significant transactions." The notice requirements for a special board meeting should be individually determined.

An example of a significant transaction is discussed in a 2000 Pennsylvania opinion. Under a corporation's stockholders' agreement, "'Significant Transactions' necessitate heightened notice and voting requirements" for board meetings. Special meetings not involving "Significant Transactions" (under the corporate governance documents) require only two days' notice unless the meeting was otherwise required, in which five days' notice is required.[10]

§ 22 Defective Notice

There is some disagreement about whether a motion that passes at a meeting for which there was defective notice is thereby rendered void or voidable.

A failure to provide a director with required notice of a special board meeting (according to a 2015 Pennsylvania Superior Court decision) "renders the actions taken at the meeting voidable—not void—and thus subject to ratification."[11] Other courts may rule differently.

A 2009 Michigan court found actions taken by a majority of a board of directors at a special meeting invalid.[12] The notice of the meeting failed to comply with the company's bylaws, according to the court.[13]

When a meeting is beset by a faulty notice, an organization should take a close look at the next meeting at how it may be able to cure its problematic decisions at the former meeting.

§ 23 LLC

A 2004 Delaware case distinguished between notice requirements for an LLC special board meeting and a corporation special board meeting.[14] The court held that members of an LLC have fewer advance special meeting notice rights than do directors of a conventional business corporation.

Other courts may take a different position.

§ 24 Waiver of Meeting

If all directors provide their written consent to a proposal that is intended to be the subject of a special meeting, the need for the special meeting is waived and the motion is approved.

Waiver of the notice requirement for a special board meeting was noted in a 2008 Texas case.[15]

OTHER COMMENT

As noted above, under *Robert's Rules*, the call of a special meeting must specify the business to be transacted at the meeting.[16] However, *Robert's Rules* also states that other procedural motions that relate to the same subject matter are in order at the meeting. For example, even though not identified in the call of the meeting, motions to adopt germane amendments, postpone consideration of the subject, and commit to a committee are permitted.

At a special meeting of a business corporation, motions secondary to the main motion (for example, germane floor amendments) may be highly significant to the outcome of the meeting. Here again, meeting rules must be reviewed to see what secondary motions are permitted.

If action is taken on matters when there was defective notice of the meeting, often that action, to be valid, must be ratified at a later proper meeting.

---

1   *See, e.g.,* Friedman v. Dolan, 2015 WL 4040806, at *10 (Del. Ch. Jan. 23, 2015). A Massachusetts case featured a shareholder who participated in a meeting by a conference call. The court noted that the bylaws did not prohibit participation in the meeting by telephone. Moreover, the minutes of the special meeting showed that the shares were in fact voted by proxy. Memorandum of Decision and Order on Plaintiffs' Motion for Partial Summary Judgment, Pasquale v. Casale, No. 021115, 2004-MBAR-559 (Mass. Super. Ct. Dec. 6, 2004). The Pennsylvania statute provides that "except as otherwise provided in the bylaws, one or more persons may participate in a meeting of . . . the board of directors of a business corporation by means of a conference telephone or other electronic technology by means of which all persons participating in the meeting can hear each other. Participation in a meeting pursuant to this Section shall constitute presence in person at the meeting." 15 Pa. Const. Stat. §1708(a).

2   Henry M. Robert III, Daniel H. Honemann, Thomas J. Balch, Daniel E. Seabold & Shmuel Gerber, Robert's Rules of Order Newly Revised § 9:31 (12th ed. 2020) [hereinafter Robert's Rules].

3   May v. National Bank of Commerce, 387 F. Supp. 2d 770, 778 (W.D. Tenn. 2004) (citing Tenn. Code Ann. § 48-18-202 (a)). Another case illustrating unanimous consent involved a board of directors approving the issuance of shares of stock in exchange for certain return of assets. APMD Holdings, Inc. v. Praesidium Med. Prof 1 Liab. Ins. Co. (Tex. App. 2018).

4   For example, see Cal. Corp. Code § 9211(c), which states, "Each director shall have one vote on each matter presented to the board of directors for action. No director may vote by proxy."

5   *In re* Sandia Tobacco Mfrs., Inc., 571 B.R. 449, 453 (Bankr. N.M. 2017) (citing the New Mexico Business Corporation Act). Similarly, in an Alaska case, the court noted that Alaska Statute § 10.06.470(c) provides that "[n]otice of a meeting need not be given to a director . . . who attends the meeting without protesting before the meeting or at its commencement the lack of notice." Brooks v. Horner, 344 P.3d 294, 300 (Alaska 2015).

6   Robert's Rules, *supra* note 2, at 91.

7   OptimisCorp. v. Waite, 2015 Del. Ch. LEXIS 222, at *129 (Del. Ch. 2015). *See also id.* at *129 n.432.

8   Kings Wharf Island Enters., Inc. v. Rehlaender, 34 V.I. 23, 29 (1996) (finding that appointment of board vacancies and other business lacked notice).

9   *See* Otk Associates, LLC v. Friedman, 85 A.3d 696, 712, 714 (Del. Ch. 2014), featuring a director who at the beginning of a full board meeting "again objected to the notice, explained that he would only participate because he believed his fiduciary duties required him to do so, and clarified that he did not intend to waive his objection to the notice by participating." Note: The trial court subsequently found inadequate meeting notice and other problems and issued a preliminary injunction.

10 Anchel v. Shea, 762 A.2d 346 (Pa. Super. Ct. 2000). The court did not find that removal from office of the CEO and president was not a "significant transaction," so heightened notice was not needed.

11 Opinion, Linde v. Linde Enters., Inc., 2015 Pa. Super. 136, at 20 (Pa. Super. Ct. 2015).

12 Innovative Adult Foster Care, Inc. v. Ragin, 776 N.W.2d 398 (Mich. Ct. App. 2009). The court quoted the Michigan Model Civil Jury Instructions, which state that "[a] special meeting held in the absence of some of the directors, without any notice to them as . . . prescribed [in the bylaws] is illegal, and the action of the meeting, although by a majority of the directors, is generally invalid." *Id.* at 407 (citing 6 Mich. Civ. Jur., Corps. § 104). The court also cited Broughton v. Jones, 120 Mich. 462, 464, 79 N.W. 691 (1899).

13 *Innovative Adult Foster Care, Inc.*, 776 N.W.2d at 398.

14 Klaassen v. Allegro Dev. Corp., 2013 Del Ch. LEXIS 275, at *15, *28 (Del. Ch. 2013). The LLC Agreement had to be considered. The court further discussed the notice that was given and what a director was aware of with respect to the specific topics for discussion. The court commented, "[T]he problem with failing to provide advance notice of a special board meeting in the manner required by the bylaws is that a director who does not receive notice cannot attend and participate in his capacity as a director." The court also stated: "Unless notice be given to each director of a special meeting of the board of directors as required by the by-laws, the meeting is illegal and action taken thereof is not binding. *Id.* at n.8. *See also* Lippman v. Kehoe Stenograph Co., 95 A. 895, 898 (Del. Ch. 1915) ("It is, of course, fundamental that a special meeting held without due notice to all the directors is not lawful, and all acts done at such meeting are void.").

15 Nord Service, Inc. v. Palter, 548 F. Supp. 2d 366 (E.D. Tex. 2008).

16 Robert's Rules, *supra note 2* § 9:13.

CHAPTER 7

Shareholders Meetings

§ 25 Electronic Means

Under most if not all state business corporation statutes, shareholders may meet by telephone.[1]

Under *Robert's Rules*, an electronic meeting "does not lose its character as a deliberative assembly . . . so long as the meetings provide, at a minimum, conditions of opportunity for simultaneous aural communication among all participating members equivalent to those of meetings held in one room or area."[2]

A Pennsylvania statute addresses shareholders meetings held by means of the internet or other electronic communication technology. The meeting must be held

> in a fashion pursuant to which the shareholders have the opportunity to read or hear the proceedings substantially concurrently with their occurrence, vote on matters submitted to the shareholders, pose questions to the directors, make appropriate motions and comment on the business of the meeting, the meeting not to be held at a particular geographic location.[3]

OTHER MEETING DETAILS

The applicable state business statute typically covers most, if not all, of the usual meeting details. For example, a Massachusetts statute provides that stockholder's meetings shall be held "within the

Commonwealth, or, to the extent permitted by the articles of organization, elsewhere in the United States."[4]

According to a Pennsylvania statute, "The bylaws of a business corporation may provide for the number and time of meetings of shareholders. Except as otherwise provided in the articles, at least one meeting of the shareholders shall be held in each calendar year for the election of directors . . . ."[5]

However, when permissible, the organization's bylaws may govern some or all of these topics.

§ 26 Proxies

The use of proxies by stockholders in stock business corporations is specifically recognized in state statutes and *Robert's Rules*.[6] This is distinguished from "voluntary associations," in which proxies are often not used or recognized.

§ 27 Waiver of Notice

Waiver of a meeting notice by an attendee is recognized in the law.

Applicable statutes and case law should be consulted to determine how an effective objection by a shareholder to a faulty notice may be made. Mere attendance and especially participation in a meeting often results in the waiver of defective notice. This is fact-sensitive and a meeting attendee should give careful attention to this issue.

§ 28 Notice of Shareholders Meeting

(NOT A SPECIAL MEETING)

The notice must include the place, date, and time of the meeting. Depending on the nature of the business to be transacted, the notice may need to specify the agenda.

Notice of a regular shareholders meeting must be in writing and comply with the organization's documents. Meeting notice requirements in the articles of incorporation and bylaws may not violate the applicable state statute.

Any shareholder may waive notice. Notice requirements for the meeting are waivable upon written consent of the shareholders. Attendance by a member may constitute a waiver of a defective notice, especially if no formal objection is raised at the beginning of the meeting. (If an objection is raised, in this writer's opinion, a request should be made to include that objection in the minutes.)

NATURE OF NOTICE

Notice requirements for a shareholders meeting are largely determined by state statute. The applicable state statute should be consulted. For example, in Pennsylvania, the notice need state only the general nature of the business to be transacted.[7] The corporation has no duty to augment the notice beyond the express requirements of the statute.[8]

In a 2015 Minnesota case, the court stated that written notice was required before any shareholders meeting unless notice was deemed to have occurred by virtue of attendance at the meeting.[9]

When certain types of action are proposed for a shareholders meeting, the notice must set out that action. For example, under an Indiana statute, when all or substantially all of a corporation's assets are to be sold, the notice must advise the shareholders that they are entitled to dissent.[10]

In a 2011 Alaska case, the court wrote that bylaws may contain any provision giving notice of a shareholders meeting if it is not in conflict with law or the articles of incorporation.[11]

Again, under the Pennsylvania statute, notice must be given to each shareholder of record entitled to vote at the meeting at least "ten days prior to the day named for a meeting that will consider a transaction . . . (relating to entity transactions) or a fundamental change . . . ."[12]

Notices pertaining to proposed bylaw amendments have their own rule in Pennsylvania statutory law:

> Notice in record form of the meeting of shareholders of a business corporation that will act on the proposed amendment must be given to each shareholder entitled to vote thereon. The notice must include the proposed amendment or a summary of the changes to be effected thereby . . . ."[13]

Similar statutorily rules apply with regard to notice to shareholders of dissolution of a corporation.[14]

EFFECT OF NOTICE FAILURE – CASE LAW EXAMPLES

In a 2015 California case, the court held that without proper notice, any action taken at a shareholders meeting was invalid and void.[15]

A 2016 Massachusetts case featured an improper shareholders meeting notice that made all actions taken at the meeting invalid. However, at a subsequent meeting, shareholders were able to ratify those actions.[16]

Each applicable state statute must be consulted.

FAILURE OR REFUSAL TO GIVE NOTICE

In Pennsylvania, should there be a failure or refusal to give shareholders notice, a Pennsylvania statute provides a remedy: "Alternative authority - If the Secretary or other authorized person neglects or refuses to give notice of a meeting, a person calling the meeting may do so."[17]

Again, each applicable state statute should be consulted.

WAIVER OF NOTICE

An alleged defective notice of a shareholders meeting was addressed in a Pennsylvania case.[18] The court cited the Pennsylvania Business Corporation Law regarding a shareholder who attends a meeting and does not object to the notice. The court referred to "Section 1705 [which] expressly provides that a shareholder is deemed to have waived defective notice where the shareholder attends a meeting and does not object to the inadequacy of the notice."[19]

In a reported federal Texas case, a sole shareholder "waived the shareholder notice requirement and called a special shareholder meeting."[20]

States handle notice waivers differently. An aggrieved shareholder should be aggressive in learning and preserving his or her rights.

§ 29 Special Meetings of Shareholders

Special meetings of the members of an organization are recognized in virtually all parliamentary references. These meetings take place between regular meetings when a matter of utmost importance or of an unusual nature needs to be considered. Special meetings of shareholders are recognized in applicable state statutes. Corporate document requirements must also be followed.

Special meetings have their own requirements with regard to notice of the meeting, what may be discussed, and what may be voted on. Under *Robert's Rules*, a session of a special meeting is normally concluded in a single meeting unless the group that is meeting schedules an adjourned meeting at the special meeting.[21]

MINUTES

Under *Robert's Rules*, minutes of a previous regular meeting may not be approved at a special meeting.[22] However, the minutes of a special meeting may be approved at the next regular meeting.

WHO MAY CALL

Special meetings of shareholders are subject to varying requirements regarding who has authority to call them. Such requirements are typically found in the state statute or the corporation's bylaws, or both. For example, a special meeting may at times be called by the president, the board of directors, or by an established percentage of the shareholder power. A provision in bylaws specifying who may call a special meeting may not be in conflict with the applicable statute.

The percentage of shareholders needed to call a special shareholders meeting differs and must be determined on a case-by-case basis. The following cases illustrate some of the differences.

In a 2015 Connecticut case, it was noted that 25% of the holders of outstanding shares of common stock may call a special meeting.[23] In a 2008 Texas case, on the other hand, it was noted that 40% of the voting power of the outstanding shares of capital stock could call a special meeting.[24]

As noted above, this is an issue addressed in state corporation statutes. For example, Florida law "permits the shareholders of ten percent or more of the common shares of a corporation to call a shareholders' meeting."[25] Under a Massachusetts statute, "[v]oting by proxy [at a special shareholders' meeting] is a legal and legitimate procedure."[26]

A New Mexico court noted that under a corporate bylaw, "a special meeting of shareholders may be called by the directors, or when the New Mexico Corporation Act confers the right to call a special meeting of the shareholders."[27]

REASONS FOR CALLING

Corporate documents and state statutes must be reviewed in each situation to see what reasons authorize the calling of a special meeting.

State corporation statutes specify many of the reasons for a special meeting. These include, among others, proposed mergers and amendments of the corporation's bylaws. Other reasons for calling a special shareholders meeting include removing current board members (with or without cause) and electing new directors. More examples from case law follow.

A 2016 Florida case involved a special shareholders meeting that was called to consider a merger.[28]

A Guam statute provided that a special meeting of shareholders may be called for any purpose at any time by the president, the board of directors, or one or more shareholders holding not less than one-fifth of the voting power of the corporation.[29]

In a 2008 Delaware state case, the court upheld the need for a special meeting for a vote of shareholders to elect directors.[30]

LACK OF NOTICE

Organizations must carefully comply with notice requirements in both statutes and their bylaws for the holding of special shareholder meetings. The case law that follows illustrate many of these requirements. They vary.

A Pennsylvania case featured a special shareholders meeting that was called without proper notice.[31] The deficiency was noted and as a result the corporation called a second special meeting. The court ruled that a properly called special meeting may ratify/affirm actions taken at a previous special meeting.[32]

The court noted that actions taken at a special shareholders meeting without proper notice are voidable, not void; decisions may be "corrected" or affirmed at the next special meeting that is properly noticed and held.[33] Of course, fraudulent activities may not be ratified.

A New York court noted that an attempt "to amend its by-laws to permit holders of 15 percent of CSX shares to call a special meeting of shareholders at any time for any purpose [is] permissible under Virginia law."[34]

A Pennsylvania state corporate statute states that unless otherwise provided in the bylaws, 20% of shares that are entitled to vote may call a special meeting of the shareholders,[35] and it may also be called by the board of directors or by such officers or other persons as may be provided for in bylaws.[36]

In a 2004 Massachusetts case, the court ruled that "even though the bylaws expressly authorize notice only by the clerk or any . . . officer designated by the Directors," the notice of a special shareholders meeting may be issued by directors.[37]

§ 30 Proxy Voting

Under a Massachusetts statute, "[v]oting by proxy [at a special share-holders meeting] is a legal and legitimate procedure."[38]

While that is the prevailing rule, the applicable state statute, including its details, should be consulted. Further discussion is beyond the scope of this book.

---

1   *See, e.g.,* Friedman v. Dolan, 2015 WL 4040806, at *10 (Del. Ch. Jan. 23, 2015). *See also* Memorandum of Decision and Order on Plaintiffs' Motion for Partial Summary Judgment, Pasquale v. Casale, No. 021115, 2004-MBAR-559 (Mass. Super. Ct. Dec. 6, 2004) (featuring a shareholder who participated in a meeting by a conference call; the court noted that the bylaws did not prohibit participation in the meeting by telephone, and the minutes of the special meeting showed that the shares were in fact voted by proxy).

2   Henry M. Robert III, Daniel H. Honemann, Thomas J. Balch, Daniel E. Seabold & Shmuel Gerber, Robert's Rules of Order Newly Revised § 9:31 (12th ed. 2020) [hereinafter Robert's Rules].

3   15 Pa. Const. Stat. § 1704(a).

4   *See* Memorandum of Decision and Order on Plaintiffs' Motion for Partial Summary Judgment, Pasquale v. Casale, No. 021115, 2004-MBAR-559 (Mass. Super. Ct. Dec. 6, 2004) (citing Section 35 of Chapter 256B; the issue in the case concerned a contested special stockholder meeting).

     Under the Pennsylvania statute, "meetings may be held at such geographic location within or without this Commonwealth as may be permitted in or fixed pursuant to the bylaws. [Otherwise] all meetings of the shareholders shall be held at the executive office of the corporation wherever situated." 15 Pa. Const. Stat. § 1704(a).

5   15 Pa. Const. Stat. § 1755. Moreover, under the Pennsylvania statute, "the bylaws may provide for . . . the time, place and manner for calling and holding meetings of the directors and executive committees and the number that constitute a quorum." 15 Pa. Const. Stat. § 7721.

6   Robert's Rules, *supra* note 2 § 45:70 ("In a stock corporation . . . where the ownership is transferrable, the voice and vote of the member also is transferable, by use of a proxy.").

7   15 Pa. Const. Stat. § 1704(c).

8   *Id.*

9   Folie v. Aging Joyfully, Inc., 2015 WL 1959854, at. *1 (Minn. Ct. App. May 4, 2015) ("The bylaws specify that waiver of the [10-day] notice requirement shall be provided in writing or by attendance at the meeting."). *See also* Opinion, Hoyt v. CollaborativeMed, LLC, No. 2015-001123 (S.C. Ct. App. Feb. 21, 2018) (featuring an allegation that failure to provide notice of a shareholders' meeting in compliance with the requirements of the corporation's bylaws was a breach of fiduciary duty).

10   Trietsch v. Circle Design Group, 868 N.E.2d 812 (Ind. Ct. App. 2007).

11   Henrichs v. Chugach Alaska Corp., 260 P.3d 1036 (Alaska 2011).

12   15 Pa. Const. Stat. §.1704(b).

13   15 Pa. Const. Stat. §.1913.

14   15 Pa. Const. Stat. §.1973 ("Notice of Meeting of Shareholders (Dissolution) (a) General Rule - Notice in record form of the meeting of shareholders that will consider the dissolution of the business corporation must be given to each shareholder of record entitled to vote thereon. The purpose of the meeting must be stated in the notice.").

15   Calpop. Com., Inc. v. Hoover (Cal. Ct. App. 2015). In addition, proper notice was not served in a meeting in which there was removal of directors. The state code required written notice of shareholders meetings.

16   Narahari v. DBLS Holdings Ltd., 65 N.E. 3d 32 (Mass. App. Ct. 2016).

17   15 Pa. Const. Stat. § 1704(d).

18   Linde v. Linde Enters., Inc., 2015 Pa. Super. 136 (Pa. Super. Ct. 2015).

19   *Id.* at 21. But, significantly, the court further noted that "since a shareholder may waive notice by attending a meeting and not objecting, one cannot say that the failure to provide a shareholder with notice of a meeting causes the actions taken at the meeting to be void *ab initio.*" *Id.*

20   Nord Service, Inc. v. Palter, 548 F. Supp. 2d 366, 369 (E.D. Tex. 2008).

21   Robert's Rules, *supra note* 2 § 9:13.

22   *Id.* at 473–74.

23   NexPoint Advisors, L.P. v. TICC Capital Corp. (D. Conn. 2015).

24   Nord Service, Inc. v. Palter, 548 F. Supp. 2d 366 (E.D. Tex. 2008). *See also* Ulloa v. Ulloa, 2012 Guam 10 (Guam 2012) (requiring 50% of shares entitled to vote and that the special meeting be called for a valid purpose according to the bylaws).

25   C.A. Cavendes, Sociedad Financiera v. Fla. Nat'l Banks, 556 F. Supp. 254, 256 (M.D. Fla. 1982) (citing Fla. Stat. § 607.084(3)(b).

26   Memorandum of Decision and Order on Plaintiffs' Motion for Partial Summary Judgment, Pasquale v. Casale, No. 021115, 2004-MBAR-559 (Mass. Super. Ct. Dec. 6, 2004) (citing Mass. Gen. Laws ch. 156B, § 41).

27   *In re* Sandia Tobacco Mfrs., Inc., 571 B.R. 449, 453 (Bankr. N.M. 2017)

(citing Section 53-11-28(c) of New Mexico's Business Corporation Act). A Utah court quoted a state statute: "A corporation shall hold a special meeting of shareholders . . . if the holders of shares representing at least 10% of all the votes entitled to be cast on any issue proposed to be considered at the proposed special meeting sign, date and deliver to the corporation's secretary one or more written demands for the meeting, stating the purpose or purposes for which it is to be held." Ha v. Trang, 380 P.3d 337, 339 (Utah Ct. App. 2016), quoting Utah Code Ann. § 16-10a-702 (LexisNexis 2013).

28   Order, Siegmund *ex rel.* Linkwell Corp. v. Bian, No. 12-62539 (S.D. Fla. 2016).

29   *See* Ulloa v. Ulloa (*In re* Chamorro Equities, Inc.), 2012 Guam 10, 12 (Guam 2012).

30   Portnoy v. Cryo-Cell Intern., Inc., 940 A.2d 43, 47 (Del. Ch. 2008). The court ordered a new special meeting in part because "stockholders cast their votes in ignorance of material facts" at the prior meeting. *See In re* Sandia Tobacco Mfrs., Inc., 571 B.R. 449, 457 n.4 (Bankr. N.M. 2017) (noting that a special meeting of shareholders, properly convened, removed a member of a board). The legality of the procedure of calling a special shareholders' meeting was discussed in Ruling and Order, No. 3:17-cv-02138 (SRU), In re China Petrochemical Dev. Corp. (D. Conn. 2018).

31   Linde v. Linde Enters., 2015 Pa. Super. 136 (Pa. Super. Ct. 2015). One of the shareholders was not given any notice of a special shareholders meeting. "[T]he general rule is well established that stockholders can ratify action of the Board of Directors which they themselves could have lawfully authorized." *Id.* at 19 (quoting Chambers v. Beaver-Advance Corp., 140 A.2d. 808, 811 (Pa. 1958)). In Espinoza *ex rel.* Facebook, Inc. v. Zuckerberg, 124 A.3d 47, 55 (Del. Ch. 2015), the court noted that under Delaware law, in the case of a special meeting, the purpose or purposes for which the meeting is called must be stated in the written notice.

32   *Linde*, 2015 Pa. Super. 136.

33   *Id.* at 20–23. The court further referenced section 1705 of the Pennsylvania Business Corporation Law.

34   Csx Corp. v. Children's Inv. Fund Management (UK), 562 F. Supp. 2nd 511 (S.D.N.Y. 2008).

35   19 Pa. Const. Stat. § 23-13. However, Section 2521 of the Pa. BCL provides that the shareholders of a registered corporation shall have no statutory right to call a special meeting. The statement commonly used by a non-registered corporation to prevent such meetings usually reads: "The shareholders of the corporation shall not be entitled to call a special meeting of the shareholders of the corporation."

36   15 Pa. Const. Stat. § 1755(b). The statute goes on to state: "At any time, upon written request of any person who has called a special meeting, it shall be the duty of the Secretary to fix the time of the meeting which, if the meeting is called pursuant to a statutory right, shall be held not more than 60 days

after the receipt of the request. If the Secretary neglects or refuses to fix the time of the meeting, the person or persons calling the meeting may do so. See Section 2521 (relating to call of special meetings of shareholders)."

37　Memorandum of Decision and Order on Plaintiffs' Motion for Partial Summary Judgment, Pasquale v. Casale, No. 021115, 2004-MBAR-559 (Mass. Super. Ct. Dec. 6, 2004) (citing Mass. Gen. Laws ch. 156B, § 41).

38　*Id.* The court cited G. L.c. 156B, §41.

CHAPTER 8

Voting and Elections at Meetings

§ 31 Voting

Under the Pennsylvania Corporation Law, an organization's bylaws may provide for "the manner of voting and the conditions upon which members may vote at general or special meetings . . . ."[1]

In a 1982 federal Florida case, the court wrote that shareholders were entitled to vote (regarding a proposed merger) by their total number of shares, not on a per capita basis.[2] This is the generally accepted rule for how shareholder voting is calculated.

Under Maine's corporation law, except for director removal, the corporation may establish greater-than-majority requirements.[3]

PROXIES BY DIRECTORS

Directors may not use proxies for directors' meetings. They must be present to vote. One reason is that "his associates are entitled to his judgment, experience and business ability."[4]

CHANGING A VOTE

The right of a shareholder to change his or her vote before the polls are closed is noted in a 2007 Delaware case.[5] Parliamentary references support this principle.

MEETING WAIVER

Under a 2004 Delaware state case, a decision may be made without the need for a meeting if all of the members of the board agree to it.[6]

This should be done in writing. One shortcoming is the loss of the sharing of ideas afforded by prior in-person debate.

§ 32 Elections

PROXIES BY SHAREHOLDERS

State law must be consulted regarding shareholders' use of proxies. For example, Delaware law permits the use of proxies by shareholders for the election of directors.[7] This is the prevailing practice.

INITIAL BOARD

Under the Pennsylvania Corporation Law, with regard to the initial corporate directors, "If the directors are not named in the articles of incorporation . . . the BCL (relating to organization meeting) provides that they [directors] shall be elected by the incorporators."[8]

Once again, the applicable state statute must be consulted.

VOTE NEEDED – CASE LAW EXAMPLES

In a 1991 federal Maryland case, the court declared that the Maryland Corporation Code overrode a bank bylaw providing that "the affirmative vote of the holders of at least 80% of the voting power of all classes of shares entitled to vote in the election of directors share be required to amend, repeal or to adopt any provision inconsistent with Sections 2.01 through 2.06 of the By-laws."[9]

In a 1995 Maryland case, federal banking law superseded Maryland statutory law in an election of directors.[10] Federal law required a majority vote for each director, while Maryland law allowed for plurality voting. The bank charter, upheld, stated that "a majority of all votes cast at any meeting of the members shall determine any question."[11] The bank noted that it was holding the election of directors in accordance with *Robert's Rules*, which require election by a majority vote.[12]

A 2017 New Mexico bankruptcy court noted, "Unless otherwise provided in the [New Mexico] Business Corporation Act, the affirmative vote of a majority of shares represented at the meeting shall be the act of the shareholders."[13]

CONTESTED ELECTION

Elections of directors by shareholders are sometimes contested. For example, a 1990 New York case, citing an earlier New York case, enunciated the following excellent summary:

If reasonable grounds exist to indicate that the election under review has not been conducted in a proper, regular or fair manner, it should not be confirmed. If the result is not free from suspicion, or is clouded in doubt, and justice demands, we [the court] may in all fairness require the parties to start over again. When right, justice and fair play require, a new election should be ordered. (Matter of Bogart, 215 A.D. 45 [213 N.Y.S. 137][)].[14]

Here again the applicable state statute regarding contested elections should be consulted.

NOMINATING COMMITTEE

Some organizations use a nominating committee to offer a slate of proposed directors.[15] Under *Robert's Rules*, the nominating committee may nominate more than one candidate for an office unless the bylaws say otherwise.[16] Individual business corporate documents, which may create a nominating committee, such as bylaws, must be consulted.

ACCEPTING THE POSITION

There is some debate about whether an elected director is required to expressly accept the position.[17] This could have an impact on when a statutory limitations period applicable to challenging an election begins to run. In this writer's opinion, good practice is for elected officers and directors to formally accept their new positions either in writing or at a business meeting.

INSPECTORS OF ELECTION

Many larger organizations appoint inspectors of election to oversee elections.[18] Their operation is described in state corporation statutes and sometimes in a corporation's internal documents. This is beyond the scope of this book.

---

1   15 Pa. Const. Stat. § 7721.

2   C.A. Cavendes, Sociedad Financiera v. Fla. Nat'l Banks, 556 F. Supp. 254, 256 (M.D. Fla. 1982).

3   Georgia-Pacific Corp. v. Great Northern Nekoosa, 731 F. Supp. 38, 41 (D. Me. 1990) (noting that under Section 611 of the Maine Business Corporation Act, "[t]he articles or bylaws may require a vote greater than a majority, may require a unanimous vote, and may specify that the stipulated percentage shall be determined with reference to the total shares entitled to vote, either as to specific issues or as to all issues which may come before the shareholders").

4   Klaassen v. Allegro Dev. Corp., 2013 WL 5967028, at *5 (Del. Ch. Nov. 7, 2013). *See also* Memorandum Opinion, Kleinberg v. Aharon, No. 12719-VCL, at *9 (Del. Ch. Feb. 13, 2017) ("As a matter of Delaware law, a director cannot act by proxy." (citing *In re* Acadia Dairies, Inc., 135 A. 846, 847 (Del. Ch. 1927)).

5   Mercier v. Inter-Tel (Delaware), Inc., 928 A.2d 786, 798 (Del. Ch. 2007). The vote concerned a proposed merger. *See also* Chapter 13, *infra*, for further discussion of this subject. In a 2018 Ohio case, a "shareholder [who] returned a proxy or voting instruction . . . but had 'second thoughts'" was given "the right to . . . change a vote on the website, by telephoning via an '800' number, by delivering a subsequently-executed proxy or by delivering a written revocation." Opinion and Order, Ratner v. Forest City Realty Tr., Inc., No. 1:18CV2605 (N.D. Ohio Nov. 26, 2018).

6   Solstice Capital II, Ltd. P'ship v. Ritz, 2004 Del. Ch. LEXIS 39, at *2 (Del. Ch. Apr. 6, 2004) ("Section 141(f) of the Delaware Code provides that '[u]nless otherwise restricted by the certificate of incorporation or bylaws, any action required or permitted to be taken at any meeting of the board of directors . . . may be taken without a meeting if *all* members of the board . . . consent in writing.'").

7   Yusufzai v. Owners Transp. Commc'n, Inc., 2008 N.Y. Slip Op. 50216(u) (N.Y. Sup. Ct. Feb. 4, 2008). Such a provision was also in the corporate bylaws.

8   19 Pa. Const. Stat. § 23.8.

9   Larkin v. Baltimore Bank Corp., 769 F. Supp. 919, 934 (D. Md. 1991).

10 Ideal Fed. Sav. Bank v. Murphy, 663 A.2d 1272 (Md. 1995). The court looked with favor on an election of board members in which candidates voted on separately with a "yes," "no," or "abstain" vote were elected. The court noted that Maryland public policy favored the presence of minority-voted shareholders but was superseded by federal law requiring a majority-vote election of each director.

11 *Id.*

12 *Id.* at 449 (citing the 1990 edition of *Robert's Rules*). "To be elected [to the board], the candidate would have to receive a majority of 'for' votes . . .; abstentions were not to be counted." *Id.*

13 *In re* Sandia Tobacco Mfrs., Inc., 571 B.R. 449, 453 (Bankr. N.M. 2017).

14 Jordan v. Allegany Co-op. Ins. Co., 558 N.Y.S.2d 806, 809 (N.Y. Sup. Ct. 1990) (quoting Matter of Kaminsky, 251 A.D. 132, 139–40, 295 N.Y.S. 989 (N.Y. Sup. Ct. 1937), *aff'd.*, 13 N.E. 2d 456 (1938)). Procedures for contesting an election are beyond the scope of this book.

15 *See, e.g.*, Rowen v. LeMars Mut. Ins. Co. of Iowa, 357 N.W.2d 579, 582 (Iowa 1984) ("A credentials committee was to investigate each candidate's eligibility and qualifications and report to the nominating committee."). *See also* Jacobs v. Yang, 2004 WL 1728521, at *4 (Del. Aug. 2, 2004). There, the board used a nominating committee, comprised of new employees and directors, who recommended board directors. It was thought that "The nominating committee ensures that the Insider Defendants . . . are incapable of controlling a director's nomination, election and continued tenure on Yahoo's board." *Id. See also In re* Scana Corp. Derivative Litig. (D.S.C. 2018) (featuring allegations by shareholders that a corporate nominating committee failed to nominate directors with relevant qualifications).

16 Henry M. Robert III, Daniel H. Honemann, Thomas J. Balch, Daniel E. Seabold & Shmuel Gerber, Robert's Rules of Order Newly Revised§46.11. (12th ed. 2020) [hereinafter Robert's Rules].

17 *See, e.g.*, Christ v. Lake Erie Distribs., Inc., 273 N.Y.S.2d 878 (N.Y. Sup. Ct. 1966) ("Election alone does not make the person elected a director; there must also be an acceptance, either express or implied." (citing Cameron v.

Seaman, 69 N.Y. 396, 398 (N.Y. 1877)). The court also cited *Robert's Rules* (presumably the edition then in effect).

18   *See, e.g.,* Portnoy v. Cryo-Cell Intern., Inc., 940 A.2d 43, 63 (Del. Ch. 2008). Further discussion of inspectors of election is beyond the scope of this text.

CHAPTER 9

Bylaw Amendments

§ 33 Significance

All prominent parliamentary references set out the process for amending bylaws. This is a crucial matter for organizations. Bylaws are a central legal document that controls how an organization operates. Therefore, the procedure for amending bylaws can have a major impact.

The detailed procedures for the adoption of bylaw amendments by nonprofits described in the parliamentary references are generally not found in the case law for business corporations. For example, unlike common practice for nonprofit organizations, there is little or no discussion in the case law about the procedure for further amending bylaws already on the floor.

Another illustration of the difference is the scope of bylaw amendments to the initial amendments permitted at the meeting. Parliamentary references for nonprofits have a number of rules on what is allowed. For example, any proposed floor amendments must be within the scope of the notice for the originally proposed bylaw amendments. In comparison, the reported case law for business corporations rarely, if ever, mentions the possibility of allowing amendments to the proposed amendments at a meeting.

Under the *Standard Code* and *Robert's Rules*, bylaw amendments go into effect immediately upon adoption unless the motion to adopt or a companion motion specifies a later date.[1]

WHAT PERCENTAGE IS NEEDED

The percentage vote needed to adopt bylaw amendments should not be taken for granted. It can differ.

Under *Robert's Rules*, for example, proposed bylaw amendments "should always prescribe the procedure for their amendment, and such provision should always require at least advance notice be given in a specified manner, and that the amendment be approved by a two-thirds vote."[2]

In contrast to *Robert's Rules*, a simple majority vote of the issued shares of a business corporation will normally be sufficient to amend bylaws. However, the corporate articles or bylaws may require a so-called super-majority of, for example, a two-thirds vote of the shares.

This principle is expressed in a 2000 New York case, in which the court stated: "It is well settled that a simple majority of shareholders is sufficient to amend corporate bylaws unless the certificate of incorporation provides otherwise."[3] As noted above, this differs from the parliamentary references for nonprofits, which typically require a two-thirds vote to adopt bylaw amendments.

A 2004 Colorado case further illustrates this concept. The court rejected an attempt to require a super-majority rather than a majority to amend bylaws.[4] The court noted that either the articles or the bylaws must authorize requiring more than majority shareholder vote to amend bylaws. A super-majority voting provision was ruled void.[5]

In a Delaware case, bylaw amendments proposed by the board of a corporation made it more difficult for stockholders to bring business before the board or nominate directors and more difficult for stockholders to call special meetings of stockholders, limited shareholders' ability to act by written consent, and required a super-majority for stockholders to amend the new bylaws.[6]

Corporate documents typically require only a majority vote to amend bylaws. As we have seen, in comparison, parliamentary references for nonprofits typically require a two-thirds vote.

WHO HAS THE AUTHORITY

In addition to the shareholders, the board of a corporation may amend bylaws if that authority is specifically authorized in the articles of incorporation, the bylaws, or the applicable statute.

For example, in deciding who had the authority to amend the bylaws, an Arkansas court quoted Arkansas statutory law:

> A. A corporation's board of directors may amend or repeal the corporation's bylaws.
>
> B. A corporation's shareholders may amend or repeal the corporation's bylaws even though the bylaws may also be amended or repealed by its board of directors.[7]

Each applicable state statute must be consulted, as must corporate documents, to determine who has the authority to amend bylaws.

A question may arise regarding how a vote is determined when amending corporate bylaws when directors also own shares. For example, in a 2004 Arkansas case, the court identified and answered this question: "The question then becomes whether, when amending the bylaws, the board of directors vote per shareholder or per share. The trial court determined the latter. We agree."[8]

ILLEGAL BYLAWS

Proposed corporate bylaws that violate state or federal statutes are void.[9]

1   American Institute of Parliamentarians, Standard Code of Parliamentary
    Procedure 240 (2012).

2   Henry M. Robert III, Daniel H. Honemann, Thomas J. Balch, Daniel E.
    Seabold & Shmuel Gerber, Robert's Rules of Order Newly Revised 56:50
    (12th ed. 2020) [hereinafter Robert's Rules]. *Robert's Rules* describes a
    lengthy detailed process to amend bylaws at sections 57:1–19 and elsewhere.
    These rules, except for the notice expectations, are rarely mentioned or
    followed in corporate case law.

3   Matter of Stile v. Antico, 707 N.Y.S.2d 227, 227 (N.Y. App. Div. 2000) (citing
    N.Y. Bus. Corp. Law § 614[b]; Model, Roland & Co. v. Indus. Acoustics Co.,
    209 N.E.2d 553 (N.Y. 1965)).

4   Harding v. Heritage Health Products Co., 98 P.3d 945, 948 (Colo. App.
    2004) ("We conclude that the trial court was correct in determining that,
    under Colorado law, either the board of directors or the shareholders could
    determine the number of directors, and that granting this power exclusively
    to the board of directors is contrary to Colorado law.") *But see* May v. R.A.
    Yancey Lumber Corp., 822 S.E.2d 358, 267 (Va. 2019) (noting that by state
    statute, certain corporate action may require more than two-thirds vote of
    the shareholders; for example, "a disposition or sale that leaves a corporation
    without a 'significant continuing business activity'").

5   Harding v. Heritage Health Products Co., 98 P.3d 945, 948 (Colo. App.
    2004).

6   Portnoy v. Cryo-Cell Intern., Inc., 940 A.2d 43, 48 (Del. Ch. 2008).

7   Taylor v. Hinkle, 200 S.W.3d 387 (Ark. 2004). The court recited the corpo-
    rate bylaws regarding amending bylaws: "These bylaws may be altered or
    amended by a vote of the majority of the holders, in good standing, of the
    fully paid-up common stock at any annual or special meeting of the stock-
    holders at which a quorum is present but notice of the proposed change
    shall be given in the call of the meeting." *Id.* at 395.

8   *Id.* at 395–96. The court noted that to allow, for example, "a person holding
    98% of the shares in a closed corporation [to] be subjugated to the will of
    other shareholders who collectively hold two percent [would cause] an
    absurd result." *Id.* at 396.

9   *See* Crown Emak Partners, LLC v. Kurz, 992 A.2d 377, 379 (Del. 2010); Kurz
    v. Holbrook, 989 A.2d 140 (Del. Ch. 2010) (conflicts with Delaware law). *See
    also* Wentworth v. Wentworth, No. 333030 (Mich. Ct. App. Oct. 17, 2017)
    ("Generally, an entity's bylaws . . . may provide for the regulation and man-
    agement of its affairs as long as the provision is not inconsistent with law or
    the articles authorizing the entity," quoting Conlin v. Upton, 881 N.W.2d 511
    (2015)).

CHAPTER 10

Plurality Voting, Tie Votes, and Abstentions

§ 34 Plurality

An election or vote on a proposition that is decided by whichever choice receives the most votes, with no choice requiring a majority of votes, is a plurality decision. For a vote to be decided by a plurality, at least three options must be simultaneously available. For example, there must be at least three candidates running for office.

Under *Robert's Rules*, plurality voting is permitted for nonprofits only when a special rule authorizes it. Further, plurality voting in an election must be authorized in an organization's bylaws.[1] Otherwise a majority vote is required.

Another method of voting, preferential voting, occurs when only one ballot is used to determine a winner, even if a majority is not obtained on the first count. This method is described in *Robert's Rules*.[2]

Business corporations must take a case-by-case approach in determining whether plurality voting is permissible or required. Among the documents and factors to consider are the organization's articles, bylaws, applicable state law, and sometimes federal preemption. There is no one answer for all situations.

AUTHORIZED

In the cases below, we see examples of determinations made based on a corporation's bylaws or a state statute. Federal law may also apply.

In a New Jersey case, the court mentioned that under the corporate bylaws, "each nominee owns stock and the proposed slate will be elected in a plurality vote."[3]

In a Delaware case, the factual background included "a contested election of directors under a plurality voting standard."[4] Another Delaware case involved a dispute that arose over the validity of a bylaw that stated that an incumbent director who received only a plurality vote (not the required majority) could continue to serve "until a successor has been elected or until the director's resignation or removal."[5]

Maryland statutory law was cited by a court when a bank used majority voting. The court stated, "In other words, section 2-404(d) [of the Maryland corporate law] was intended to make it easier to elect directors [using a plurality vote] and to reduce the number of failed elections."[6]

TAKES A MAJORITY

Other courts require a majority vote. Once again, this must be determined on a case-by-case basis. Examples follow.

In a Maryland case, a bank informed voters for directors that they were required to vote by written ballot and that they should vote "for," "against," or "abstention" as to each candidate.[7] To be elected, the candidate would have to receive a majority of "for" votes; abstentions were not counted.[8]

The court went on to state that applicable federal regulatory law prohibited a plurality vote and also overrode Maryland statutory provisions that permitted plurality voting.[9]

In a 2000 Delaware case, a bank's bylaws required majority voting to elect a director—"not merely a plurality of the votes cast, as is more usually the case."[10]

§ 35 Tie Votes

A deadlock results if a matter requires a majority vote for approval but a majority cannot be obtained because an equal number of votes are cast by each side.

Under the two leading parliamentary references for nonprofits, the following rules apply: A tie vote is considered a lost vote. Stated differently, a majority vote in the affirmative is required to adopt a motion. A tie vote rejects the proposal.[11] A tie vote is only to be followed by further voting when there is an election or if two or more alternate propositions are on the table.[12] Under the *Standard Code* for nonprofits, when there is a tie vote in an election, the choices "may be voted on again until one is elected," or the tie may be broken in another way if the assembly so decides.[13]

Tie votes may take place at either a meeting of directors or a meeting of shareholders. Tie votes of directors occur when an even number of directors vote for and against a pending motion or other matter. Tie votes of shareholders occur when an equal number of owned or controlled shares are voted for and against a measure.

Sometimes the corporate documents provide for the manner of breaking a tie. Otherwise, if the methods of breaking a tie are inadequate or disputed, a court is sometimes asked to intervene by one or both parties.

In a 2017 Delaware case, the facts featured a 3–3 board split on critical issues. The court noted that under the applicable Delaware statute, a deadlock exists when "the directors are so divided respecting the management of the affairs of the corporation that the required vote for action by the board of directors cannot be obtained."[14]

The consequences of tie votes are noted in other legal cases. For example, in a New York case, the president of a corporation sought permission to bring a suit but there was a tie vote. The court treated this as a refusal of permission by the directors.[15]

For a deadlock to occur, a tie vote must actually take place. It may not be merely speculated about. For example, the court in a New York case made clear that preventing action by the president required an actual vote by the board rejecting the proposed action by either a majority vote against or a 50–50 deadlock.[16]

OTHER COMPLICATIONS FROM TIES

As mentioned above, without an actual meeting, a tie vote by shareholders may not be assumed. Consequently, there can be no deadlock when the potentially tying shareholder fails to attend a shareholders meeting. For example, a court stated in a 2004 South Dakota case,

"A shareholder may not boycott a shareholders' meeting and claim deadlock just because he does not believe that his position or arguments will carry the day."[17]

A particular corporate bylaw amendment mentioned in a New York case states that "in the event of a tie vote, [a sitting director] may designate a third director to vote on items that do not require unanimous director approval."[18]

A New Mexico case featured a motion that was made and seconded for a corporation to issue stock pursuant to an exercise of subscription rights. The motion resulted in a tie vote, but the stock was issued anyway. Litigation followed.[19]

STATUTORY REMEDY

Some, if not all, states provide a statutory remedy in the event of a tie shareholders vote for a board election. Examples follow.

In a New York case involving an LLC, the court appointed a fifth director to break a 2–2 deadlock.[20]

In a 2018 California case, where the shareholders each held 50% of the shares, the court ordered the shareholders to hold an annual meeting to elect directors.[21]

In another California case, the court noted that a statute "grants the provisional director all the rights and powers of a director and the right to vote at such meetings until the deadlock is broken or he is removed by the Court or the shareholders."[22]

A South Dakota case featured a winner being determined by "drawing of lots under such procedure that all rights of the candidates involved in such tie are adequately safeguarded."[23]

§ 36 Abstentions

An abstention occurs when an eligible voter participating in a meeting deliberately decides not to vote. Under *Robert's Rules*, the chair of a meeting does not ask who abstains[24] from a vote. Generally, the abstainer's lack of a vote in nonprofits is ignored in calculating a result. Otherwise, an abstention would have the unintended consequence of being a "no" vote.

Under *Robert's Rules*, counting an abstention as a "no" vote denies a meeting participant the right to maintain a neutral position.[25] It also makes it more difficult for those supporting a proposition to overcome the abstention and obtain an affirmative vote of the requisite number of those present.

Under the *Standard Code*, a member has the right to abstain from voting on any motion. And a person *must* abstain at a nonprofit meeting if he or she has a sufficient financial or other applicable conflict of interest in the outcome of a vote.[26]

HOW TREATED

The rule in the traditional parliamentary authorities—that an abstention is ignored when calculating an outcome—is not necessarily the procedure followed in the business corporation arena. Business corporations differ in how they handle abstentions. Some ignore them, while others treat them as a "no" votes. Each situation has to be determined. How an abstention is handled can have a major impact on the outcome of a vote.

IGNORED

There is disagreement among courts on the impact of an abstention in determining the result of a corporation vote. Here are two examples where abstentions were not counted:

In a New York case that involved proxy voting at a shareholders meeting, abstentions were not counted when determining whether a majority voted for a measure.[27]

Abstentions were also not counted in a 1991 Maryland federal case.[28] "[T]he weight of authority establishes that 'votes cast' do not include abstentions."[29]

COUNTED AS A "NO" VOTE

Other case law illustrates a contrary view—that an abstention has the effect of a "no" vote. For example, in a Massachusetts federal case (in a different context), the court indirectly treated an abstention as a definite "no" vote.[30] The court stated:

> Shareholders who abstained from the merger vote are in no different a position than those who voted against the merger; they too are entitled to recover. The Massachusetts case demonstrates that acquiescence is not to be inferred from abstention.[31]

The court relied heavily on the Massachusetts Business Corporation statute:

> The statute in question makes clear that those who abstained on the merger vote should be in no different position than those who voted against the merger, because merger approval required the affirmative vote of a majority of each class entitled to vote. M.G.L. c. 156B, § 78(c)(1)(iii). Abstention was as effective as voting against the merger.[32]

Once again, how abstentions are treated when calculating the outcome of a vote must be determined on a case-by-case basis. They may, of course, have a major impact on the result of a vote. In this writer's opinion, it is good practice for a corporation to decide in advance, subject to any requirements, how abstentions are to be handled.

Of note, a Delaware court began its opinion by quoting "[t]wo scholars of Delaware corporate law" for the proposition that an abstention is counted as a "no" vote when "a majority of the shares present and entitled to vote on the subject matter is needed to pass a measure."[33] As previously mentioned, this is contrary to how the parliamentary references for nonprofits would normally treat this situation.

The Federal Reserve, it was reported in a Florida case, warned that a "holding company board of directors' minutes should clearly note [a bank director's] abstention from all policymaking decisions regarding the bank."[34]

Parliamentary references for nonprofits support ignoring abstentions when calculating a vote. However at times this may not be done by business corporations, who often count an abstention as a "no" vote. Each situation must be researched.

PROTECTION FROM LIABILITY

Having abstained from voting is sometimes offered as a rationale for why someone is not responsible or liable for the results of a vote and its consequences. For example, this argument was attempted but rejected in a 2013 Ohio case.[35] A transaction was approved at a meeting, with one of the eventual litigants abstaining from the vote. That person raised the abstention as a defense in the subsequent lawsuit. The court rejected this argument because "given the facts of this case [the person that had a role in negotiations], abstention on the transaction does not entitle them to summary judgment."[36]

This defense was also raised in a 2021 Delaware case.[37] The Court there noted:

> While "Delaware law already prescribes that a director who plays *no* role in the process of deciding whether to approve a challenged transaction cannot be held liable on a claim that the board's decision to approve that transaction was wrongful," this is "not an invariable rule." The "cookie-cutter step [of not voting] is not sufficient to establish a successful abstention defense" where for example, "certain members of the board of directors

conspire with others to formulate a transaction that is later claimed to be wrongful."

PROXIES

The wording on a proxy and directions to the proxy holder can be crucial in deciding whether an abstention is ignored or counted as a "no" vote. The proxy should be crafted to anticipate and clarify this situation.

Examples from case law follow.

In a 2005 Delaware case, it was held that if a proxy holder has been directed to abstain, that vote is to be counted as a "no" vote.[38] On the other hand, if the owner directs the proxy holder not to vote, the failure to vote is not counted as a "no" vote.

A Delaware court looked to a business corporation statute[39] and a Delaware Supreme Court decision[40] in holding that if a proxy gives limited authority and directs the proxy holder not to vote on an issue, then the failure to vote is not counted as a "no" vote and is ignored in the calculation. This is how the parliamentary references for nonprofits would treat the situation.

Yet, in a New York federal case decided under Delaware law, it was held that approval of a merger required that "a majority of the out-standing stock of the corporation entitled to vote thereon shall be voted for the adopting of the agreement."[41] The court further decided that "in the context of a proxy vote to approve a merger agreement, an abstention (or any vote other than 'yes') is tantamount to a 'no' vote."[42]

Rule 14(a)-4 of the Exchange Act requires that a security held for proxy have a box that allows for an abstention on each separate matter (other than elections to office).[43]

1   Henry M. Robert III, Daniel H. Honemann, Thomas J. Balch, Daniel E. Seabold & Shmuel Gerber, Robert's Rules of Order Newly Revised 44.11 (12th ed. 2020) [hereinafter Robert's Rules] ("A rule that a plurality shall elect is unlikely to be in the best interests of the average organization."); American Institute of Parliamentarians, Standard Code of Parliamentary Procedure 140–41 [hereinafter Standard Code]. Both parliamentary references discourage elections by plurality vote since arguably they thwart the will of the majority.

2   Robert's Rules, *supra* note 1 §§ 45:62, 45:62-72. This must be set forth in the bylaws. This subject is beyond the scope of this book.

3   Bolger v. First State Fin. Servs., 759 F. Supp. 182, 192 (D.N.J. 1991).

4   Mercier v. Inter-Tel (Delaware), Inc., 929 A.2d 786 (Del. Ch. 2007).

5   Kistefos AS v. Trico Marine Services, Inc., 2009 WL 1124477, at *2–3 (Del. Ch. Apr. 14, 2009). The court found a decision on the issue to be premature at the time.

6   Badlands Tr. Co. v. First Fin. Fund, Inc., 224 F. Supp. 2d 1033, 1036 (D. Md. 2002). The court concluded, "I find that the Fund's bylaw requiring a majority of shares outstanding to elect a director is invalid under Maryland law." *Id.* at 1038.

7   Ideal Fed. Sav. Bank v. Murphy, 663 A.2d 1272 (Md. 1995).

8   *Id.* at 1273.

9   *Id.* Incidentally, the Bank's conduct of the meeting and method of voting for directors were governed by *Robert's Rules*.

10   North Fork BanCorp., Inc. v. Toal, 825 A 2d 860, 861 (Del. Ch. 2000).

11   Robert's Rules, *supra* note 1 §§ 4:56, 44:12.

12   Standard Code, *supra* note 1, at 142.

13   *Id.* at 308.

14   Kleinberg v. Aharon, 2017 Del. Ch. LEXIS 24, at *32 (Del. Ch. Feb. 13, 2017) (citing Del. Code Ann. tit. 8, § 226(a)). Moreover, the court went on to say, "The deadlock must be a product of 'genuine, good faith divisions.'" *Id.* (quoting Shawe v. Elting, LLC., 2015 WL 4874733, at *28 (Del. Ch. Aug. 13, 2015)).

15   Sterling Indus. v. Ball Bearing Pen Corp., 84 N.E.2d 790 (N.Y. 1949).

16   *See* Hellman v.Hellman, 2008 MU Slip. Op. 28086, 19 Misc. 3d 695. A significant point made by the court was that if a director wants to establish a deadlock, he or she must demonstrate that the deadlock actually took place at a meeting—that it wasn't just speculation outside a meeting.

17   Lien v. Lien, 674 N.W. 2d 816, 824 (S.D. 2004).

18 Davis v. Rondina, 741 F. Supp. 1115, 1117 (S.D.N.Y. 1990).

19 Graham v. Cocherell, 733 P. 2d 370 (N.M. Ct. App. 1987).

20 Belardi-Ostroy, Ltd. v. Am. List Counsel, Inc., 2016 NY Slip Op 30727 (U), at 9 (N.Y. Sup. Ct. 2016) (stating that "a board meeting can take place and deadlock can be resolved by the newly appointed fifth Director"). A deadlock in this case was not grounds for dissolution. *But see* Memorandum Opinion, Acela Invs. LLC v. DiFalco, No. 2018-0558-AGB (Del. Ch. May 17, 2019) (board of managers deadlock resulted in a court-ordered corporate liquidation).

21 Opinion, Ielmini v. Patterson Frozen Foods, Inc., No. F073377 (Cal. Ct. App. Sept. 12, 2018).

22 ANNRHON, Inc. v. Lesinski, 17 Cal. App. 4th 742, 753 (Cal. Ct. App. 1993). The court noted that a "provisional director must be an impartial person who is neither a shareholder nor a creditor of the corporation, nor related to any other director or any judge of the court which is appointing the director." *Id.* at 751. Further, the court wrote, "The statutory language grants the provisional director all the rights and powers of a director and the right to vote at such meetings, until the deadlock is broken or he is removed by the court or the shareholders." *Id.* at 753.

23 Lien v. Lien, 674 N.W. 2d 816, 824 (S.D. 2004), quoting S.D. Codified Laws § 47-5-6(3).

24 Robert's Rules, *supra* note 1 § 4:35.

25 *Id.* at 403.

26 Standard Code, *supra* note 1, at 140.

27 Bank of New York Co., Inc. v. Irving Bank Corp., 531 N.Y.S.2d 730 (N.Y. Sup. Ct. 1988). The proxy included a check box for "abstention." The court commented on Section 613(c) of the New York Not-For-Profit Corporation Law but did not find it "persuasive."

28 Larkin v. Baltimore Bancorp., 769 F. Supp. 919, 921 n.1 (D. Md. 1991). The court cited a line of cases in support of this proposition. And also, interestingly, section 43 of the 1990 edition of *Robert's Rules* was mentioned. "Management also contends that abstentions should be counted as 'votes cast' within the meaning of Md.Corps. [*sic*] & Ass'ns Code Ann § 2-506(a). If that were correct, the contention would be the sword which cut the Gordian knot since it would render academic all of the other issues presented. However, the contention does not have merit . . . . Common sense supports the majority view. Certainly, a Bank stockholder who purposely chose to abstain on Dissidents' proposals did not intend to cast, in effect, a vote in favor of Management on the issues." *Id.*

29 *Id.*

30 Pavlidis v. New England Patriots Football Club, 675 F. Supp. 696, 700 (D. Mass. 1987).

31   *Id.* The Court went on to cite Brannistein v. Devine, 149 N.E.2d 628 (Mass. 1958) ("The Court ruled that abstention could not be considered acquiescence where the shareholders could have considered a 'no vote to be pointless.'").

32   *Pavlidis*, 675 F. Supp. at 700.

33   Licht v. Storage Tech. Corp., 2005 WL 1252355 n.1 (Del. May 6, 2005) ("[I]n determining whether a [shareholder] proposal has passed in a circumstance where the vote is required 'a majority of the shares present and entitled to vote on that subject matter,' abstentions . . . are to be treated as shares present and 'entitled to vote on the subject matter.' Applying that standard, the abstention would be counted as a 'no' vote . . . ." (citing R. Franklin Balotti & Jessee A. Finklesteon, The Delaware Law of Corporation and Business Corporations § 7.25, at 7-51 (2004))).

34   Net First Nat. Bank v. First Telebanc Corp., 834 So. 2d 944, 946 (Fla. App. 2003).

35   Order Granting in Part and Denying in Part Defendants Lee Moran's and Asha Morgan Moran's Motion for Partial Summary Judgment, Miller v. Morgan (*In re* Antioch Co. Litig. Trust) (S.D. Ohio Aug. 2, 2013).

36   *Id.* at 19. Defendants cited *In re* Tri-Star Pictures, Inc. Litig., 1995 Del. Ch. Lexus 27 (Del. Ch. 1995), where a Delaware Court applying Delaware Law found that a director's abstention from voting to approve a contested transaction shielded the director from liability predicated on the board's decision to approve the board's transaction. The *Miller* court, distinguishing the cases, stated: "However, in reaching this conclusion, the court recognized that no 'per se rule unqualifiedly and categorically relieves a director from liability solely because that director refrains from voting on the challenged transaction . . . . Rather, the court's finding of no liability was based on the particular facts of the case. Specifically, that the directors had not 'played any role, open or surreptitious, in formulating, negotiating, or facilitating the transaction complained of.' . . . [T]he court in *Gesoff v. IIC Indus., Inc.*, 902 A.2d 1130, 1166 (Del. Ch. 2006), held that just because a director did not vote on the contested transaction did not absolute [*sic*] him from liability where he was closely involved with the challenged transaction from the very beginning." *Id.*

37   Memorandum Opinion, *In re* CBS Corp. Stockholder Class Action & Derivative Litig. 2020-0111-JRS, at 152 (Del. Ch. Jan. 27, 2021; corrected Feb. 4, 2021) (citations omitted), https://courts.delaware.gov/Opinions/Download.aspx?id=315980.

38   Licht v. Storage Tech. Corp., 2005 WL 1252355 (Del. May 6, 2005).

39   *Id.* (citing Del. Code Ann. tit. 8, § 216(2)).

40   *Id.* (citing Berlin v. Emerald Partners, 552 A.2d 482 (Del. 1988)). However, the court drew some significant distinctions: "Given that the Supreme Court included abstentions among the shares entitled to vote, it is implicit in the Supreme Court's opinion that an abstention and a vote withheld because

of the absence of any instruction are materially different for purposes of Delaware law, and that an abstention, whether accomplished in person or through a proxy holder following his principal's instructions, is part of the 'voting power present.'"

41   Mony Group v. Highfields Capital Mgmt., 368 F.3d 138 (2nd Cir. 2004).

42   *Id.*

43   *In re* Real Estate Assocs. Ltd. P'ship Litig., 223 F. Supp. 2d 1142 (C.D. Cal. 2002). *See also* Greenlight Capital, L.P. v. Apple, Inc., 2013 WL 646547, at *6 (S.D.N.Y. Feb. 22, 2013) in which the court refers to Section 14 of the Exchange Act, which governs shareholder proxy solicitations for publicly traded companies. *Id.* (citing 17 C.F.R. § 240.14a-4(a)(3)). "Rule 14a-4(b)(1), governing the proxy form, requires that shareholders be given 'an opportunity to specify by boxes a choice between approval or disapproval of, or abstention with respect to *each separate matter referred to therein as intended to be acted upon*." *Id.* (quoting 17 C.F.R. § 240.14a-4(b)(1)).

Postponements and Adjournments

§ 37 Postponements of Meetings

Traditional parliamentary references commonly recognize motions at a meeting to postpone a pending motion to later in that same meeting or to a subsequent meeting. However, in this chapter, "postponement" refers to something different: delaying an already scheduled shareholders or directors meeting to a later time or date. This situation can lead to controversy. There is considerable case law on the subject, especially in relation to a board postponing a scheduled shareholders meeting.

The parliamentary authorities for nonprofits are largely silent on this subject. The *Standard Code* comments about officers or directors who fail to call a meeting in accordance with the organization's documents.[1] The *Standard Code* suggests that a member of a group consult applicable (nonprofit) statutes to determine if the group is in compliance with the law with respect to calling a meeting.

A sample of the case law offers the following rulings about postponements.

In a 1996 Louisiana case, the facts pertained to the failure of a a motion to postpone a vote about a financial commitment.[2]

Three postponements of a shareholders meeting to a later date was featured in a 2015 Illinois case.[3]

In a 2012 Guam case, the court distinguished between a corporate officer setting a date for an annual meeting and postponing a meeting already scheduled.[4] The Guam court quoted a Louisiana case:

> The *Silverman* court narrowly held that the directors in that case did not possess authority to postpone the annual meeting indefinitely after they had already made the call and notice for the annual meeting . . . . The *Silverman* case is distinguishable because this case did not involve a postponement of a meeting that had already been called.[5]

In a 1997 Delaware case, the court strongly disfavored directors postponing a scheduled shareholders meeting:[6] "directors of a corporation could not postpone the scheduled annual meeting as long as it was possible to hold the meeting at the time originally scheduled. The Court pointed out [in another case] that a different holding would 'authorize directors to change a meeting date for any year, at any time in advance of a meeting, for any reason of convenience to the directors, provided no fraud, bad faith, or improper motion was shown.'"[7]

BALANCING OF INTERESTS

A court may balance a legitimate need (and motive) to postpone a meeting against the harm that a delay could cause. For example, in a Delaware Chancery Court decision, a board attempted to postpone a shareholders meeting at which an incumbent director was to be reelected.[8] The court found that an unacceptable reason for postponement and enunciated the following rule.

"The burden of persuasion, however, must be upon those seeking to postpone the annual meeting to show that the postponement is in the best interests of the stockholders."[9]

This concept of protecting shareholders' interests when management attempts to postpone a meeting was featured in a 2002 Delaware Chancery Court decision in which the court found that no significant shareholder interest was served by a postponement.[10]

The reverse gave rise to another Delaware Chancery Court opinion: a stockholder unsuccessfully sought postponement of an annual stockholders meeting.[11]

In still another Delaware case, the court grappled with the equities implicated by a board announcing that a special meeting of the shareholders would be postponed.[12] An annual meeting was postponed indefinitely based on the board's announcement. Citing a line of cases, the court decided that the board's stated reason for the postponement of the shareholders meeting was inequitable.[13]

BOARD DISCRETION

The authority and decision of a board to postpone a scheduled shareholders meeting is a potentially serious matter and open to court scrutiny. Whether such a postponement is justifiable is fact-specific and decided on a case-by-case basis. Examples from the case law follow.

The business judgment rule was invoked in a Delaware case involving a majority of "disinterested" directors successfully voting to postpone a stockholder meeting to a new record date.[14]

The court reasoned that "[b]ecause that decision is not the product of any inequity or unfairness, but rather is one that permits a full and fair vote, the court will review it under the business judgment rule."[15]

In a 2007 Delaware case, directors were found to have discretion to effect a "short" postponement of a shareholders meeting while it was in the process of voting for a merger.[16]

Against the backdrop of a perceived tender offer, a board voted to cancel an annual shareholders meeting.[17] The board unsuccessfully argued in the resultant Massachusetts federal case that bylaw provisions allowing for the calling of special meetings overrode bylaw provisions regarding a date certain for the annual meeting. The court held that "the Board's reliance on the special meeting provision . . . was misplaced, and that the Board's purported meeting change was *ultra vires* and, therefore, invalid."[18]

A 2011 court in Delaware opined on whether a board was exercising its fiduciary duties by postponing a special meeting of shareholders.[19] The board's stated reason was to allow shareholders an opportunity to "receive and digest material information or a change in recommendation" in a matter in which stockholder approval was requisite.[20]

A 1995 Delaware Chancery Court allowed a board to postpone a special shareholders meeting by amending the corporation's bylaws.[21] The new bylaw "extended by 35 days to 60 days the minimum time for calling a stockholder-initiated special meeting." The court decided that the directors' response to a threat (amending the bylaws) was justified. The board was, in the court's view, fulfilling "its duties to the shareholders to seek out the best value reasonably available."[22]

§ 38 Adjournments

The two cited parliamentary references discuss motions to adjourn a meeting by a majority vote. Usually this is a routine motion made when it is obvious that a meeting is coming to a close. A motion may also be made to adjourn at a specific time. Under *Robert's Rules*, a motion "to adjourn again and again when nothing has happened to justify renewal of such a motion" is frivolous and dilatory and may not be introduced.[23]

Under the *Standard Code*, if a motion to adjourn is offered but further business needs to be addressed, the presiding officer should inform the members of the situation.[24] Nevertheless, the members still have the right to vote for or against an adjournment.

Adjournment of a shareholders meeting may be routine. For example, some information gathering or verifying of proxies may be handled during a short break. This is sometimes called a "recess." Other adjournments can be longer. After an adjournment, the reconvened meeting continues with business where it left off.

In some situations, the presiding officer has the discretion to call an adjournment. In other business organizations, an adjournment is a matter requiring the formality of a vote of the attendees.

RECONVENE

Under *Robert's Rules*, when an adjourned meeting reconvenes, the meeting continues from the point where it had left off, including consideration of the question that was on the table at the time of the postponement.[25] The meeting minutes are first read. The implicit right of shareholders to reconvene a shareholders meeting was noted in a 2015 Illinois case.[26] Often an adjournment is sought to allow a matter or situation to be studied and discussed at the reconvened meeting.

VALIDITY

If not handled properly, an adjournment can create controversy. An adjournment should not be used to exploit others or to gain an unfair advantage. Further, it should be made clear to all attendees whether in fact an adjournment has been called. There can be misunderstandings among attendees if a formal motion to adjourn is not made and a vote is not taken, but instead are assumed. Therefore, in this writer's opinion, good practice requires a motion and a vote.

Case law shows the potential pitfalls of an adjournment and controversies that can arise.

A Delaware case involved a bylaw that gave the corporation's president discretion to adjourn a meeting of the stockholders.[27] This practice is fairly common but has the potential to create problems.

A 2017 Texas case considered a situation where no motion or vote to adjourn a meeting occurred,[28] yet one of the shareholders thought that an adjournment had been called. In his absence, business was conducted. Litigation over whether or not an adjournment had taken place ensued.

Other controversies can arise. For example, it was reported in a Florida federal case that because of lack of a quorum, a postponement of a shareholders meeting was attempted by a motion and second. The motion was called out of order by the chair.[29] A similar situation is reported in a Virginia Supreme Court case.[30] In that case there was a motion and a second to adjourn a meeting, but the chair ruled the motion out of order.

In a 2012 Delaware case, the validity of an adjournment of a shareholders meeting by the presiding president was challenged.[31]

In an unusual New York case, an adjournment was called because of overcrowding of the meeting room. The meeting was adjourned to a later date to allow for a bigger room. In supporting the adjournment, the court stated:

> There is no evidence that the adjournment was made
> on considerations other than inadequacy of space, and

safety of those attending from danger of fire and possible physical harm through jostling and the collapse of flooring and stairwell. There is absolutely no evidence that the adjournment was called for the purpose of thwarting the wishes of the shareholders . . . . The Court holds that the action of adjournment taken by the Chairman ... was proper under the circumstances existing.[32]

IMPACT OF THE SEC

The SEC may have an impact on shareholder adjournments. For example, in a 2007 Delaware case, the court referred to an SEC "unwritten policy" regarding shareholder voting on adjournment of meetings.[33] Under that decision, the SEC encourages issuers to seek stockholders' preapproval of an adjournment.

In a Maryland federal case, an SEC ruling took precedence over a motion to adjourn.[34] At an annual shareholders meeting, a motion and a second were made to adjourn.[35] The chair ordered an adjournment without taking a vote, declaring that the SEC required the adjournment.[36] Those who disagreed claimed, without success, that the motion to adjourn should have been put to a vote.[37]

EFFECT OF AN ADJOURNMENT

Under the two cited parliamentary references, when there is an adjournment, a new meeting date and time should be announced in the meeting at the time of the adjournment. Additional notice is usually not required, according to the parliamentary references, but in this writer's opinion there are good reasons to give additional notice. The rules requiring a business corporation to give a fresh meeting notice must be determined.

In a 1987 Delaware state case, the court quoted the state statute:

When a meeting is adjourned to another time or place, unless the bylaws otherwise require, notice need not be given of the adjourned meeting if the time and place thereof are announced at the meeting at which the adjournment is taken. At the adjourned meeting the corporation may transact any business which might have been transacted at the original meeting. If the adjournment is for more than 30 days, or if after the adjournment a new record date is fixed for the adjourned meeting, a notice of the adjourned meeting shall be given to each stockholder of record entitled to vote at the meeting.[38]

As seen above, the same business that would have been transacted at the original meeting may be undertaken at the adjourned meeting.[39]

State business corporation statutes now typically address adjournments of both regular and special meetings. Specifics are added if directors are being elected by shareholders. For example, a Pennsylvania statute directs as follows:

Adjournments - Adjournments of any regular or special meetings may be taken but any meeting at which directors are entitled to be elected shall be adjourned only from day to day, or for such longer periods not exceeding 15 days each as the shareholders present and entitled to vote shall direct, until the directors have been elected.[40]

OTHER EXAMPLES

In a 1966 New York case, the court acknowledged the right of shareholders to adjourn a meeting.[41] And, in a 2002 Delaware case, it was noted that a trial court ordered a company to immediately adjourn a shareholder meeting and thereafter reconvene to preserve the established date of the identity of the shareholders originally entitled to vote.[42]

---

1   American Institute of Parliamentarians, Standard Code of Parliamentary Procedure 110 (2012). [hereinafter Standard Code].

2   Olinde v. 400 Group, 686 So. 2d 883, 887 (La. Ct. App. 1996).

3   Order, Conrad Black Capital Corp. v. Horizon Publ'ns, Inc., No. 1-13-2116, at *6–7 (Ill. App. Ct. 2015). No meeting was ever held.

4   Ulloa v. Ulloa (*In re* Chamorro Equities, Inc.), 2012 Guam 10 (Guam 2012).

5   Silverman v. Gilbert, 185 So. 2d 373, 376 (La. Ct. App. 1966).

6   Aprahamian v. HBO & Co., 531 A.2d 1204, 1206 (Del. Ch. 1987).

7   *Id.*

8   *Id.*

9   *Id.* at 1207. The court noted that stockholders meeting dates can be changed for cause. *Id.* at 1208 (citing Steinberg v. Am. Bartram, 76 F. Supp. 426 (W.D. Pa. 1948); Tweedy, Browne & Knapp v. Cambridge Fund, Inc., 318 A.3d 635 (Del. Ch. 1974)); *id.* at 1207 (stating that "an annual meeting could be postponed if necessary in the interests of the stockholders" (citing *Steinberg*, 76 F. Supp. 426; Thompson v. Enstar, 509 A. 2d 578 (Del. Ch. 1984))).

10   McKesson Corp. v. Derdiger, 793 A.2d 385 (Del. Ch. 2002). "In *Aprahamian*, on the eve of HBO's scheduled shareholder meeting, the management of HBO decided to postpone the meeting upon receiving information from their proxy solicitor that a group of insurgent shareholders might defeat the management's proposals." The plaintiff challenged that delay and this Court held that the postponement served no significant stockholder interest and directed that the annual meeting be convened as scheduled. . . ." *Id.* at 390 (citing Aprahamian v. HBO & Co., 531 A.2d 1204 (Del. Ch. 1987)).

11   Third Point LLC v. Ruprecht, 2014 WL 1922029, at *14 (Del. Ch. May 2, 2014). The court summarized the shareholder request to postpone the annual meeting in part as follows: "Plaintiffs assert that the balance of the equities weighs in their favor in this instance because any harm from a brief postponement of the annual meeting is outweighed by the serious harm, both monetary and otherwise, that would have to be incurred if the Court eventually decides the Rights Plan was invalid and requires the Company to hold another director election." However, the Shareholder's motion for a preliminary injunction was denied.

12   MM Cos., Inc. v. Liquid Audio, Inc., 813 A.2d 1118 (Del. 2003).

13   *Id.* at 1132 (stating that "the incumbent Board timed its utilization of these

otherwise valid powers to expand the size and composition of the . . . board. . . . As this Court held more than three decades ago, 'these are inequitable purposes, contrary to established principles of corporate democracy . . . and may not be permitted to stand.'" (quoting *Schnell v. Chris-Craft, Indus., Inc.*, 285 A.2d 437, 439 (Del. 1971))).

14 *In re* MONY Grp., Inc. S'holder Litig., 853 A.2d 661 (Del. Ch. 2004).

15 *Id.* at 666–67. The court upheld the board decision to postpone the stockholder meeting and to set a new record date.

16 Mercier v. Inter-Tel (Delaware), Inc., 929 A.2d 786 (Del. Ch. 2007).

17 ER Holdings, Inc. v. Norton Co., 735 F. Supp. 1094 (D. Mass. 1990).

18 *Id.* at 1100.

19 *In re* Compellent Techs, Inc. S'holder Litig, 2011 Del. Ch. LEXIS 190, at *25 (Del. Ch. Dec. 9, 2011). Note: The Court offered speculation but did not provide an answer.

20 *Id.*

21 Kidsco, Inc. v. Dinsmore, 674 A.2d 483, 485 (Del. Ch. 1995) (citing MAI Basic Four, Inc. v. Prime Computer, Inc., 1989 Del. Ch. LEXIS 69 (Del. Ch. June 13, 1989); Hartnett, V.C., No. 10868, 1989 WL 63900 (Del Ch. July 13, 1989) ("upholding directors' 42 day postponement of previously scheduled annual stockholders meeting to give directors 'reasonable time to find alternatives to [a] new offer'")).

22 *Id.* at 497.

23 Henry M. Robert III, Daniel H. Honemann, Thomas J. Balch, Daniel E. Seabold & Shmuel Gerber, Robert's Rules of Order Newly Revised § 39:1-4 (12th ed. 2020) [hereinafter Robert's Rules].

24 Standard Code, *supra* note 1, at 79–80.

25 Robert's Rules, *supra* note 24 § 9:19.

26 Order, Conrad Black Capital Corp. v. Horizon Publ'ns, Inc., No. 1-13-2116, at *6-7 (Ill. App. Ct. 2015). *See* Chen v. Howard-Anderson, 87 A.3d 648, 655 (Del. Ch. 2014) (featuring a board that agreed to reconvene by telephone to allow a business matter to be evaluated in the interim).

27 Gentili v. L. O. M. Med. Int'l, Inc., 2012 Del. Ch. LEXIS 183, at *8–9 (Del. Ch. Aug. 13, 2012).

28 Florie v. Reinhart, 2017 Tex. App. LEXIS 1798, at *12–14 (Tex. App. Mar. 2, 2017). The court found that even though "there was no vote on a motion to adjourn, nor was there any discussion about adjournment," the director who left reasonably believed that the meeting was over and that subsequent business was invalid.

29 C.A. Cavendes, Sociedad Financiera v. Fla. Nat'l Banks, 556 F. Supp. 254, 256 (M.D. Fla. 1982). The party contending the motion to adjourn was in order cited *Robert's Rules*.

30   Levisa Oil Corp. v. Quigley, 234 S.E. 2d 257 (Va. 1977).

31   *Gentili*, 2012 Del. Ch. LEXIS 183, at *8. Some stockholders left, others stayed, and the corporate counsel "purported to countermand that adjournment. After a brief recess, the vote [for directors] was taken." The court noted that the challenged directors (who were elected) had a choice to have a hearing on the validity of the adjournment or seek a new stockholders meeting held under court supervision.

32   Jordan v. Allegany Co-op Ins. Co., 558 N.Y.S.2d 806, 808 (N.Y. 1990) (distinguish its facts from those of *In Re* Dollinger Corp., 274 N.Y.S.2d 285 (N.Y. 1966).

33   Mercier v. Inter-Tel (Delaware), Inc., 929 A.2d 788, 792 (Del. Ch. 2007). *See also id.* at 792 n.11. (citing a transcript of a roundtable discussion that includes discussion of SEC unwritten rules).

34   Larken v. Baltimore Bancorp, 769 F. Supp. 919 (D. Md. 1991).

35   *Id.*

36   *Id.*

37   Larkin v. Baltimore Bancorp, 769 F. Supp. 919, 927–28 (D. Md. 1991) ("The very purpose of the adjournment was to protect the fairness and integrity of the proxy process by enabling all the stockholders, not simply those present at the meeting, to cast a fully informed vote on the questions of control of the Bank. This purpose would have been defeated by permitting dissidents to end the meeting . . . .").

38   Aprahamian v. HBO & Co., 531 A.2d 1204, 1208 (Del. Ch. 1987) (citing Del. Code Ann. tit. 8, § 222(c)).

39   *Id.*

40   15 Pa. Const. Stat. § 1755(c).

41   *In re* Dollinger Corp., 274 N.Y.S.2d 285 (N.Y. 1966). The court went on to say, "It would seem that if the right of adjournment at an annual meeting is given to the shareholders in the absence of a quorum, it is idle to urge that they are without this prerogative when they assemble as a duly constituted body for effective action. It is the shareholders' meeting, the owners of the company, who have the right to make a decision on a question of adjournment, and not of the president who has only the duty of presiding." *Id.* at 287.

42   McKesson Corp. v. Derdiger, 793 A.2d 385, 390 (Del. Ch. 2002).

CHAPTER 12

Ratification of Vote

§ 39 General Principles

Ratification takes place when a vote is reaffirmed by a new vote at a later business meeting.

Excluded from this chapter is shareholder ratification of corporate activity or proposed activity. Also excluded is shareholder ratification of board actions.[1]

Under traditional parliamentary references, a motion to ratify is used to confirm or validate action that may not be approved until the assembly meets again—for example, when there was "[an] action improperly taken at a regular or properly called meeting at which no quorum was present."[2]

Also under traditional nonprofit parliamentary references, if no notice of the proposed ratification was given to attendees, a two-thirds vote is required. However, in a New York case involving a business corporation, it was held that only a majority vote of the stockholders was needed to ratify discontinuance of a previously approved derivative suit.[3] This is an example of the procedural differences that exist at times between parliamentary references for non-profits and many of the rules for business corporations. Nonprofits typically require a two-thirds vote for ratification, in contrast to corporate voting practice, which may require only a majority vote.

LACK OF NOTICE AT A PRIOR MEETING

Caution must be exercised when there has been a failure to meet notice-of-meeting requirements—especially in relation to special meetings. Such a failure may have an impact on ratification votes at the next meeting. Each jurisdiction's law has to be researched to determine how this may be done.

The problems this can cause are revealed by a 1998 Delaware case.[4] A director was not given notice of a special board meeting. A ratification vote was presented at a subsequent special meeting, before which a different director failed to receive adequate meeting notice.

A Pennsylvania case featured a shareholders meeting that was held despite a lack of notice.[5] One of the motions at the meeting called for removal of a director, and one party claimed in litigation that vote was "null and void."[6] The court disagreed, finding that the lack of notice rendered the actions taken only voidable.[7] Therefore, at a subsequent meeting, the same resolutions were validly passed and ratified.[8] The director was reelected by a passed resolution.[9]

The same court concluded:

> [W]e see no reason why a voidable shareholders' resolution may not be ratified at a subsequent, valid shareholders' meeting, where the shareholders were fully informed of what they are asked to ratify and where no action was taken to avoid the earlier resolution.[10]

OTHER CASE LAW EXAMPLES

The case law turns in different ways.

In a 2015 Delaware case, the court held that "stockholder ratification of a self-dealing transaction must be accomplished formally by a vote at a meeting of stockholders or by written consent in order to shift the standard of review that otherwise would apply to such a transaction."[11]

In a 2012 Delaware case, subsequent written consents were not sufficient to ratify election of challenged directors.[12]

---

1   Shareholder ratification of prior board action may also raise issues as to the propriety of the prior board action. Those issues are similarly beyond the scope of this book. *See, e.g.*, Memorandum Opinion, Sciabacucchi v. Liberty Broadband Corp., No. 11418-VCG (Del. Ch. May 31, 2017).

2   Henry M. Robert III, Daniel H. Honemann, Thomas J. Balch, Daniel E. Seabold & Shmuel Gerber, Robert's Rules of Order Newly Revised § 10:54 (12th ed. 2020) [hereinafter Robert's Rules]. Under *Robert's Rules*, four other instances where another meeting is required to ratify a prior action are "(a) action taken at a special meeting with regard to business not mentioned in the call of that meeting; (b) action taken by officers, committees, delegates, subordinate bodies, or staff in excess of their instructions or authority . . ., (c) action taken by a local unit that requires approval of the state or national organization; or (d) action taken by a state or national society subject to approval by its constituent units."

3   Syracuse Television Inc. v. Channel 9 Syracuse, Inc., 275 N.Y.S.2d 190, 195 (N.Y. 1966).

4   Moore Bus. Forms, Inc. v. Cordant Holdings Corp., 1998 WL 71836 (Del. Ch. Feb. 4, 1998) (*cited in* Klaassen v. Allegro Dev. Corp., 106 A.3d 1035, 1045 n.67 (Del. 2014)). As the *Klaassen* court noted, "Moore involved a formal board resolution adopted at a special meeting from which one director was absent because he had received no notice. Thereafter, at a second special meeting (with the excluded director in attendance) the board purported to ratify its earlier resolution. The Court of Chancery held that the board action could not be ratified because it was undertaken at a special meeting of which one director had no notice. That is not this case. Here, the Allegro board did not take any official action to terminate [the CEO] until the November regular meeting at which [the CEO] was present." *Klaassen*, 106 A.3d at 1045 n. 67.

5   Linde v. Linde Enters., Inc., 118 A.3d 422 (Pa. Super. Ct. 2015). The court noted that a void resolution has no legal effect whatsoever and therefore cannot be ratified. *Id.* at 431. A voidable resolution is "valid until annulled." *Id.* at 432 (quoting Black's Law Dictionary 1604 (8th ed. 2004)). The failure to provide proper notice of a special shareholders meeting caused the resolutions passed at the meeting to be voidable, but not void. *Id.* at 433 (citing 15 Pa. Const. Stat. Ann. § 1705(b)).

6   Linde v. Linde Enters., Inc., 118 A.3d 422 (Pa. Super. Ct. 2015).

7   *Id.*

8   *Id.*

9   *Id.*

10   *Id.* at 437 (citing Koprowski v. Wistar Inst. of Anatomy and Biology, 1993 WL 106466 (E.D. Pa. 1993)).

11   Espinoza *ex rel.* Facebook, Inc. v. Zuckerberg, 124 A.3d 47 (Del. Ch. 2015) (citing section 228 of the Delaware General Corporation law at 49). For a discussion on whether a shareholder ratification vote should operate to extinguish a duty of loyalty claim, see *In re* Wheelabrator Techs., Inc. S'holders Litig., 663 A.2d 1194 (Del. Ch. 1995).

12   Gentili v. L. O. M. Med. Int'l, Inc. 2012 WL 3552685, at *3 (Del. Ch. 2012). The court noted that there was no previous board action to ratify.

CHAPTER 13

Removal of Directors

§ 40 General Methods

There are three methods for removing a sitting director;

- removal by a court of competent jurisdiction,
- removal by the shareholders, and
- removal by the other board members.

Directors may also resign.

§ 41 Removal by the Court

Courts have jurisdiction under state law to remove a sitting director. This is illustrated in reported cases in Delaware, California, and Arkansas.

In a 2011 Delaware case, the court noted that Delaware law authorizes

> the Court of Chancery to "determine the validity of any election, appointment, removal, or resignation of any director or officer of any corporation, and the right of any person to hold or continue to hold such office. . . ."[1]

In a 2015 California case, the court noted that under state law, the court has discretion to remove a director for fraudulent acts, dishonesty, or "gross abuse of authority."[2]

In a 2004 Arkansas case, the court cited a state statute: "The circuit court of the county where a corporation's principal office . . .

is located may remove a director from office in a proceeding commenced either by the corporation or by its shareholders holding at least ten percent (10%) of the outstanding shares of any class . . . ."[3]

§ 42 Removal by the Shareholders

Since it is common for board members to be elected by the shareholders, it only stands to reason that shareholders also have the authority to remove directors. This is illustrated in the statutory and case law. Typically, removal may be with or without cause. The percentage vote needed to remove a director varies and must be researched for each situation.

For example, in a 2008 Nevada federal case, the court noted that "[t]wo-thirds of the shareholders of a corporation may vote to remove a director[4] from office . . . ."[4]

Shareholder agreements often include provisions setting out the procedure for removing a director.[5]

WITH OR WITHOUT CAUSE

A director may be removed with or without cause, depending on the circumstances. Examples follow.

In a 1987 Delaware case, it was mentioned that the motivation for a removal without cause is irrelevant.[6]

In a 1997 New York federal case, it was noted that under a state statute, "[r]emoval [for cause] may be effected by the shareholders. . . . An action to remove a director for cause, however, may be brought only by the attorney general or by the holders of ten percent of the outstanding shares."[7]

The statutory authority of the shareholders for removal was enunciated by a 2010 Delaware court:[8] "Section 141(k) [of the Delaware

General Corporation Law] now provides, with certain exceptions, that any director or the entire board of directors may be removed, with or without cause, by the holders of a majority of the shares entitled to vote at an election of directors."[9] It was also noted by the court that under the same statutory provision, shareholders may vote to remove directors only if they may vote to elect directors.[10]

Once again, applicable state law and corporate documents must be consulted to see what applies.

DUE PROCESS

When the removal of a director is for cause, due process and/or other procedures usually come into play. Therefore, removal of a director for cause is far more complex than removal without cause.

For example, under a 2002 Delaware case, when the governing documents permit, removal for cause, certain due process is required.[308]: "A 'for cause' removal of a director requires that the individual be given (i) specific charges for his removal, (ii) adequate notice, and (iii) a full opportunity to meet the accusation."[11]

The law of the particular state and the specific circumstances must be researched to determine the applicability and implementation of due process and cause.[12]

WRITTEN CONSENT

Written consent may be used to remove a director in some situations. For example, the court in a 2004 Delaware case held that removal of directors by shareholders may be accomplished by written consent of a majority of stockholders—a stockholders meeting is not required.[13] Written consent by shareholders was held by another 2012 Delaware case to be valid and effective to remove board members.[14]

§ 43 Removal by the Board

Removal of directors is usually done by shareholders. There is a split of legal authority on whether other directors may remove a sitting director. State business corporation law controls and must be consulted. Corporate documents may also play a role.

Under certain circumstances, a board may remove one of its own members. A 2003 Indiana case featured a director being removed by a vote of the other board members, even though the director was elected by the shareholders.[15] The authority of the board must be evaluated in each situation.

In the 1997 New York federal case mentioned above regarding removal of directors by shareholders, the court also noted that if the certificate of incorporation or a bylaw adopted by the shareholders so provides, a director may be removed by the other directors.[16]

Differences in board removal authority are illustrated in two other cases. In a 2002 Indiana case, the court ruled that a state statute allows directors to remove other directors by a majority vote with or without cause (unless the articles state otherwise).[17] But a court in a 2012 federal case in Michigan decided that under Michigan corporation law, only shareholders may remove a director.[18]

§ 44 Written Consent

Removal of a director without cause, according to a Delaware case, may be effectuated by the unanimous consent of all directors, without a meeting.[19] This issue must be evaluated on a case-by-case basis based on the law in the applicable jurisdiction.

If removal with cause is involved and due process is required, in this writer's opinion, simple written consent by other board members without more action would usually not suffice.

§ 45 Resignation

Board members may resign. There is some discussion about the appropriate procedure. For example, there is a question about whether a resignation needs to be formally accepted by the rest of the board.

Under the *Standard Code*, no formal acceptance is necessary (unless otherwise stated in the bylaws) and the resignation is effective immediately unless otherwise specified.[20]

Under *Robert's Rules*, the power to appoint or elect an officer or director carries with it the power to accept a resignation. When the bylaws grant the board authority to control the organization's affairs between meetings of the assembly, the board has the authority to accept resignations.[21]

A 2005 Massachusetts case involved directors who voted to accept the resignation of the person who was both president and a director.[22]

In this writer's opinion, formal acceptance of a director's resignation by the remaining directors avoids confusion and is the better practice.

---

1   Genger v. TR Investors, LLC, 26 A.3d 180, 183 n.2 (Del. 2011) (citing Del. Code Ann. tit. 8, § 225).

2   Opinion, Bathas v. McCluskey, No. G050228 (Cal. Ct. App. Oct. 28, 2015). It was further noted that "[a] court will not generally remove a director for alleged misconduct during a term of office if the director is reelected." The court cited Brown v. N. Ventura Road Dev. Co., 216 Cal. App. 2d 227 (Cal. Ct. App. 1963), and Remillard Brick Co. v. Remillard Dandini Co., 109 Cal. App. 2d 405, 423 (Cal. Dist. Ct. App. 1952).

3   Taylor v. Hinkle, 200 S.W.3d 387, 396 (Ark. 2004) (quoting Ark. Code Ann. § 4-27-809). "The circuit court . . . may remove a director [if it finds] that (1) the director engaged in fraudulent or dishonest conduct, or gross abuse of authority or discretion, with respect to the corporation and (2) removal is in the best interest of the corporation." *Id.* (quoting Ark. Code Ann. § 4-27-

809).

4   Advanced Optics Electronics, Inc. v. Robins, 633 F. Supp. 2d 1237 (D.N.M., 2008), p. 1236 Citing Nevada statutes §78.335 and §78.650.

5   *See, e.g.*, Davis v. Rondina, 741 F. Supp. 1115, 1124 (S.D.N.Y. 1990). The court noted that both the shareholders agreement and the bylaws of the corporation provided that the removal of officers could only be done where "an eighty-nine percent shareholder vote is required for . . . election or removal of officers or directors and establishing the number of directors." *Id.* at 1117.

6   Insituform of N. Am., Inc. v. Chandler, 534 A.2d 257 (Del. Ch. 1987).

7   Mgmt. Techs., Inc. v. Morris, 961 F. Supp. 640, 650 (S.D.N.Y. 1997). The court cited Section 706 of The New York Business Corporation Law.

8   Kurz v. Holbrook, 989 A.2d 140, 156 (Del. Ch. 2010). An Iowa court in 2012 relied on Delaware law. "[A] director may be removed without cause at any time under Delaware Law. Del. Code §141(k). A decision whether to re-elect or remove a board member is completely within the rights of shareholders." Rusch v. Midwest Indus. Inc., 2012 WL 1564704, at *5 (N.D. Iowa 2012).

9   Kurz v. Holbrook, 989 A.2d 140, 156 (Del. Ch. 2010).

10   *Id.*

11   S ssen v. Allegro Dev. Corp., 2013 Del Ch. LEXIS 275, at *15, *28 05 A.2d 904, 912 (Del. Ch. 2002) (citing Campbell v. Loew's, Inc., 134 A.2d 852, 859 (Del. Ch. 1957)). The court also added that "the same [due process] is true whether the action is taken at a meeting of stockholders or by written consent." Id. (citing Bossier v. Connell, 1986 Del. Ch. LEXIS 511, at *15 (Del. Ch. Nov. 12, 1986)).

      However, a 2018 Delaware court distinguished the need for due process for removing a corporate director for cause from removing a manager of an LLC. To do the latter, due process was not required since it was not specifically required in the partnership agreement. Letter opinion, A & J Capital, Inc. v. Law Office of Krag, No. 2018-0240-JRS (Del. Ch. July 18, 2018).

12   Superwire.com, Inc. v. Hampton, 805 A.2d 904, 912 (Del. Ch. 2002).

13   Unanue v. Unanue, 2004 WL 2521292, at *7 (Del. Ch. Nov. 3, 2004) (citing Del. Code Ann. tit. 8, § 228(a)). The court noted, again, "that the holders of a majority of a company's stock may remove a director with or without cause." *Id.* (citing Del. Code Ann. tit. 8, § 431(k)).

14   Memorandum Opinion, Keyser v. Curtis, No. 7109-VCN (Del. Ch. 2012). Written consents were also used by stockholders to remove a director in Salamone v. Gorman, 106 A.3d 354 (Del. 2014) (featuring a voting agreement that stated, "all stockholders agree to execute any written consents required to remove a director").

15   Murray v. Conseco, Inc., 795 N.E.2d 454 (Ind. 2003). However, the corporation had no provisions regarding removal of directors. The directors in question were elected by the shareholders as a whole, not by a separate

voting group. (The court did not state what vote percentage was required.)

16   Mgmt. Techs., Inc. v. Morris, 961 F. Supp. 640, 650 (S.D.N.Y. 1997) ("Removal may be effected by the shareholders or, if the Certificate of Incorporation or a by-law adopted by the shareholders so provides, by the board of directors." (citing N.Y. Bus. Corp. L. § 706(a)). In Memorandum Opinion, Frechter v. Zier, No. 12038-VCG (Del. Ch. Jan. 24, 2017), the court upheld the Delaware statute (Section 141(k) of title 8) providing that a director may be removed by the holders of a majority of shares, and it held that a corporate bylaw requiring a vote of at least two-thirds of the shares for removal violated the state law.

17   Murray v. Conseco, Inc., 766 N.E. 2d 38 (Ind. App. 2002).

18   Petroleum Enhancer, LLC v. Woodward, 690 F.3d 757, 769 (6th Cir. 2012) ("[T]here is simply no basis to deviate from Michigan's settled rule that a director cannot be removed by other directors.").

19   Solstice Capital II, Ltd. P'ship v. Ritz, 2004 WL 765939, at *1 (Del. Ch. Apr. 6, 2004).

20   American Institute of Parliamentarians, Standard Code of Parliamentary Procedure 265 (2012).

21   Henry M. Robert III, Daniel H. Honemann, Thomas J. Balch, Daniel E. Seabold & Shmuel Gerber, Robert's Rules of Order Newly Revised § 47:57 (12th ed. 2020).

22   Lampert v. Gallant, 19 Mass. L. Rptr. 283 (Mass. 2005).

CHAPTER 14

Indemnification

§ 46 Major Procedural Considerations

"Indemnification," in this chapter, refers to a business corporation paying for or reimbursing a director for the director's legal defense necessitated by, and possibly liability arising from, a claim or suit. The liability must be sufficiently related to or arising from the director's corporate position. This chapter discusses common voting procedures when indemnification is being considered at a board meeting. Neither *Robert's Rules* nor the *Standard Code* specifically mentions this subject.

The principal procedural considerations concerning indemnification that a corporation should be sensitive to are the following:

- A majority vote by the other directors is required.
- Usually, but not always, a quorum of directors is required for the vote.
- Directors with a personal interest in the situation may not vote.
- Under certain circumstances, such as when there is no quorum, an independent lawyer issues a written opinion.
- Shareholders may have the right to vote (excluding those with a personal interest).

In each situation, which of these procedural factors apply at a meeting should be evaluated.

This is an area largely if not entirely controlled by the applicable state statute and internal corporate documents.[1] For example, a 2007 California court, in considering this question, referred to the California statute then in effect, which provided:

Any indemnification under this section [requires]:

> (1) A majority vote of a quorum consisting of directors who are not parties to such proceeding.
>
> (2) If such a quorum of directors is not obtainable, by independent legal counsel in a written opinion.
>
> (3) Approval of the shareholders . . .with the shares owned by the person to be indemnified not being entitled to vote thereon.
>
> (4) The court [to so order].[2]

In another example, Wisconsin's statute governing indemnification was mentioned in a 2010 Wisconsin case. The statute provided that

> the director seeking indemnification shall select one of the following six means for determining the right to indemnification:
>
> (1) a majority vote of a quorum of disinterested directors; (2) independent legal counsel; (3) a panel of three arbitrators; (4) an affirmative vote of the shares (but not the shares of any shareholder interested in the litigation); (5) court order . . .; or (6) any other method provided for in any additional right (not applicable here).[3]

§ 47 Need for a Quorum

If a quorum cannot be obtained because too many participants have a conflict of interest or for other legally recognized reasons, a lesser number may still be able to make a determination regarding indemnification. Examples from the case law that illustrate these complexities follow.

Under a Illinois statute, a majority vote may approve indemnification even with less than a quorum voting.[4] The court noted "that any determination that indemnification is proper shall be made "by the majority vote of the directors who are not parties to such action, suit or proceeding, *even though less than a quorum*."[5]

This subject was discussed in an Oregon case. A bank's Articles of Incorporation stated that indemnification could be decided "[b]y the Board of Directors by a majority vote of a quorum consisting of directors who are not or were not parties to the action, suit or proceeding . . . ."[6]

A California federal case involved a board that had three members, but only two were present at a meeting. This constituted a quorum and the board voted in favor of indemnification.[7]

A 2000 New York case featured a 59% owner of corporate shares whose vote was deemed sufficient to approve indemnification (of legal expenses) under the state's Business Corporation Law.[8]

A Kansas case denied recovery on an indemnification claim; it discussed bad faith and the success of the litigation.[9] A Kansas statute allows for a majority vote even if there is less than a quorum.[10]

---

1   Creel v. Ecolab, Inc. (Del. Ch. 2018) ("[C]ompanies often provide indemnification to their directors and officers in their charters, bylaws, or other

agreements.").

2   Aimers v. ILive, Inc., No. B193313 (Cal. Ct. App. May 15, 2007) (citing Section 317).

3   Ehlinger v. Hauser, 785 N.W.2d 328 n.28 (Wis. 2010) (citing Wis. Stat. §180.0855). In an earlier California federal case decided in 1988, the court summarized the statute at that time differently: "[I]ndemnification [must] be authorized by (1) majority vote of disinterested directors, or (2) majority vote of disinterested shareholders, or (3 court order." PLM, Inc. v. Nat'l Union Fire Ins. Co. of Pittsburgh, Pa., 848 F.2d 1243 (Cal. 1988). The PLM court denied indemnification to the corporate directors for failure to meet the statutory requirements.

4   See Order, Santella v. Kolton, No. 05 CH 018591, at 24 (Ill. App. 2017).

5   Id.

6   Heine v. Bank of Oswego, 144 F. Supp. 3d 1198, 1206 (D. Or. 2015). The Court cited Richard A. Rossman, Matthew J. Lund & Kathy K. Lochmann, A Primer of Advancement of Defense Costs: The Rights and Duties of Officers and Corporations, 85 U. Det. Mercy L. Rev. 29, 31 (2007).

7   In re Landmark Land Co. of Carolina, Inc., 76 F.3d 553, 559–60 (4th Cir. 1996) (citing Am Bar Ass'n, Model Bus. Corp. Act Ann., introductory cmt. to chapter 8, at 1082 (3rd ed. 1987 supp.)). The court mentioned an instance of the board of directors meeting to discuss and vote on indemnification. The board consisted of five members. "At the time of the meeting, the fifth director had resigned and had not yet been replaced. The other four members of the board were present, constituting a quorum. . . . [Two of the directors] voted in favor of indemnification and [the other two directors] abstained from the vote." Id. at 560. The court noted that under Cal. Corp. Code § 317(b)(1), for a corporation to determine indemnification, there must be: "(1) A majority of a quorum consisting of directors who are not parties to such proceeding[;] (2) If such a quorum of directors is not obtainable by independent legal counsel in a written opinion[; and] (3) Approval of the shareholders . . ., with the shares owned by the person to be indemnified not being entitled to vote thereon." Id.

8   Pilipiak v. Keyes, 185 Misc. 2d 636, 640 (N.Y. Sup. Ct. 2000).

9   IAS Partners, Ltd. v. Chambers (In re Metcalf Assocs.-2000, L.L.C.), 213 P.3d 751 (Kan. Ct. App. 2009). The criteria used in finding for or against indemnification is beyond the scope of this book. Under the Kansas statute (Kan. Stat. 17-6305(d): "Indemnification of a director or officer is determined (1) by a majority vote of the directors who are not parties to such action, suit or proceedings, even though less than a quorum; (2) by a committee of such directors designated by majority vote of such directors, even though less than a quorum; (3) if there are no such directors, or if such directors so direct, by independent counsel in a written opinion; or (4) by the stockholders."

10 IAS Partners, Ltd. v. Chambers (In re Metcalf Assocs.-2000, L.L.C.), 213 P.3d 751 (Kan. Ct. App. 2009).

Appendix

Each state has its own statutes addressing business corporation meeting procedures. Selected but not all provisions of the Pennsylvania statute are shown here for illustration. (The reader should be aware that they could be revised or repealed after publication of this book.) Each applicable state statute must be independently researched.

CONDUCTING A MEETING

Pennsylvania
15 Pa. C. S. A. § 1709

§ 1709. Conduct of shareholders meeting

(a) Presiding officer.- There shall be a presiding officer at every meeting of the shareholders. The presiding officer shall be appointed in the manner provided in the bylaws or, in the absence of such provision, by the board of directors. If the bylaws are silent on the appointment of the presiding officer and the board fails to designate a presiding officer, the president shall be the presiding officer.

(b) Authority of the presiding officer.- Except as otherwise provided in the bylaws, the presiding officer shall determine the order of business and shall have the authority to establish rules for the conduct of the meeting.

(c) Procedural standard.- Any action by the presiding officer in adopting rules for and in conducting a meeting shall be fair to the shareholders.

(d) Closing of the polls.- The presiding officer shall announce at the meeting when the polls close for each matter voted upon. If no announcement is made, the polls shall be deemed to have closed upon the final adjournment of the meeting. After the polls close, no ballots, proxies or votes, nor any revocations or changes thereto, may be accepted.

WAIVER OF NOTICE OF SHAREHOLDER MEETING

Pennsylvania
15 Pa. C. S. A. § 1705

§ 1705. Waiver of notice

(a) General Rule.- Whenever any notice is required to be given under the provisions of this subject or the articles or bylaws of any business corporation, a waiver filed thereof which is filed with the secretary of the corporation in record form, signed by the person or persons entitled to the notice, whether before or after the time stated therein, shall be deemed equivalent to the giving of the notice. Neither the business to be transaction at, nor the purpose of a meeting need be specified in the waiver of notice of the meeting.

(b) Waiver by attendance.- Attendance of a person at any meeting shall constitute a waiver of notice of the meeting except where a person attends a meeting for the express purpose of objecting, at the beginning of the meeting, to the transaction of any business because the meeting was not lawfully called or convened.

ACTION BY SHAREHOLDERS WITHOUT A MEETING

Pennsylvania
15 Pa. C. S. A. § 1766

§ 1766. Consent of shareholders in lieu of meeting

(a) Unanimous consent.- Unless otherwise restricted in the bylaws, any action required or permitted to be taken at a meeting of the shareholders or of a class of shareholders of a business corporation may be taken without a meeting if a consent or consents to the action in record form are signed, before, on or after the effective date of the action by all of the shareholders who would be entitled to vote at a meeting for such purpose. The consent or consents must be filed with the minutes of the proceedings of the shareholders.

(b) Partial consent.- If the bylaws so provide, any action required or permitted to be taken at a meeting of the shareholders or of a class of shareholders may be taken without a meeting upon the signed consent of shareholders who would have been entitled to cast the minimum number of votes that would be necessary to authorize the action at a meeting at which all shareholders entitled to vote thereon were present and voting. The consents shall be filed in record form with the minutes of the proceedings of the shareholders.

(c) Effectiveness of action by partial consent.- An action taken pursuant to subsection (b) to approve a transaction under Chapter 3 (relating to entity transactions) shall not become effective until after at least ten days' notice of the action has been given to each shareholder entitled to vote thereon who has not consented thereto. Any other action may become effective immediately, but prompt notice that the action has been taken shall be given to each shareholder entitled to vote thereon that has not consented. This subsection may not be relaxed by any provision of the articles.

QUORUM OF AND ACTION BY DIRECTORS

Pennsylvania
15 Pa. C. S. A. § 1727

§ 1727

(a) General rule.- Unless otherwise provided in the bylaws, a majority of the directors in office of a business corporation shall be necessary to constitute a quorum for the transaction of business, and the acts of a majority of the directors present and voting at a meeting at which a quorum is present shall be the acts of the board of directors.

(b) Action by consent.- Unless otherwise restricted in the bylaws, any action required or permitted to be approved at a meeting of the directors may be approved without a meeting if a consent or consents to the action in record form are signed, before, on or after the effective date of the action by all of the directors in office on the date the first consent is signed. The consent or consents must be filed with the minutes of the proceedings of the board of directors.

QUORUM - SHAREHOLDERS MEETING

Pennsylvania
15 Pa. C. S. A. § 1756

§ 1756. Quorum

(a) General rule.- A meeting of shareholders of a business corporation duly called shall not be organized for the transaction of business unless a quorum is present. Unless otherwise provided in a bylaw adopted by the shareholders:

(1) The presence of shareholders entitled to cast a least a majority of the votes that all shareholders are entitled to cast on a particular matter to be acted upon at the meeting shall constitute a quorum for the purposes of consideration and action on the matter.

(2) The shareholders present at a duly organized meeting can continue to do business until adjournment notwithstanding the withdrawal of enough shareholders to leave less than a quorum.

(3) If a meeting cannot be organized because a quorum has not attended, those present may, except as otherwise provided in this subpart, adjourn the meeting to such time and place as they may determine.

(4) If a proxy casts a vote or takes other action on behalf of a shareholder on any issue other than a procedural motion considered at a meeting of shareholders, the shareholder shall be deemed to be present during the entire meeting for purposes of determining whether a quorum is present for consideration of any other issue.

(b) Exceptions.- Unless otherwise provided in a bylaw adopted by the shareholders, those shareholders entitled to vote who attend a meeting of shareholders:

(1) At which directors are to be elected that has been previously adjourned for lack of a quorum, although less than a quorum as fixed in this section or in the bylaws, shall nevertheless constitute a quorum for the purpose of electing directors.

(2) That has been previously adjourned for one or more periods aggregating at least 15 days because of an absence of a quorum, although less than a quorum as fixed in this section or in the bylaws, shall nevertheless constitute a quorum for the purpose of acting upon any matter as set forth in the notice of the meeting if the notice states that those shareholders who attend the adjourned meeting shall nevertheless constitute a quorum for the purpose of acting upon the matter.

QUORUM OF A BOARD MEETING

Pennsylvania
15 Pa. C. S. A. § 1727

§ 1727. Quorum of and action by directors

(a) General rule.- Unless otherwise provided in the bylaws, a majority of the directors in office of a business corporation shall be necessary to constitute a quorum for the transaction of business, and the acts of a majority of the directors present and voting at a meeting at which a quorum is present shall be the acts of the board of directors.

(b) Action by consent.- Unless otherwise restricted in the bylaws, any action required or permitted to be approved at a meeting of the directors may be approved without a meeting if a consent or consents to the action in record form are signed before, on or after the effective date of the action by all of the directors in office on the date the first consent is signed. The consent or consents must be filed with the minutes of the proceedings of the board of directors.

INTERESTED DIRECTORS OR OFFICERS; QUORUMS

Pennsylvania
Pa. C. S. A. § 1728

(a) General Rule.- [See Pennsylvania statute for all other provisions.]

(b) Quorum.- Common or interested directors may be counted in determining the presence of a quorum at a meeting of the board that authorizes a contract or transaction specified in subsection (a).1

USE OF CONFERENCE- TELEPHONE OR OTHER ELECTRONIC TECHNOLOGY

Pennsylvania
15 Pa. C. S. A. § 1708

§ 1708. Use of conference telephone or other electronic technology

(a) Incorporators and directors.- Except as otherwise provided in the bylaws, one or more persons may participate in a meeting of the incorporators or the board of directors of a business corporation by means of conference telephone or other electronic technology by means of which all persons participating in the meeting can hear each other. Participation in a meeting pursuant to this section shall constitute presence in person at the meeting.

(b) Shareholders.- Except as otherwise provided in the bylaws, the presence or participation, including voting and taking other action, at a meeting of shareholders or the expression of consent or dissent to corporate action by a shareholder by conference telephone or other electronic means, including, without limitation, the Internet, shall constitute the presence of, or vote or action by, or consent or dissent of the shareholder for the purposes of this subpart.

SPECIAL MEETING OF SHAREHOLDERS

ACTION BY DIRECTORS

VOTING RIGHTS

Pennsylvania
15 Pa. C. S. A. § 1729

§ 1729. Voting rights of directors

(a) General rule.- Unless otherwise provided in a bylaw adopted by the shareholders, every director of a business corporation shall be entitled to one vote.

(b) Multiple and fractional voting.- Any requirement of this subpart for the presence of or vote or other action by a specified percentage of directors shall be satisfied by the presence of or vote or other action by directors entitled to cast the specified percentage of the votes that all voting directors in office are entitled to cast.

ACTION BY SHAREHOLDERS - MAJORITY VOTE

Pennsylvania
15 Pa. C. S. A. § 1757

§ 1757. Action by shareholders

(a) General rule.- Except as otherwise provided in this title or in a bylaw adopted by the shareholders, whenever any corporate action is to be taken by vote of the shareholders of a business corporation, it shall be authorized upon receiving the affirmative vote of a majority of the votes cast by all shareholders entitled to vote thereon and, if any shareholders are entitled to vote thereon as a class, upon receiving the affirmative vote of a majority of the votes cast by the shareholders entitled to vote as a class.

(b) Changes in required vote.- Whenever a provision of this title requires a specified number or percentage of votes of shareholders or a class of shareholders for the taking of any action, a business corporation may prescribe in a bylaw adopted by the shareholders that a higher number or percentage of votes shall be required for the action.

[See other provisions of the Pa. statute for expenses]

CONDUCT OF A SHAREHOLDERS MEETING

Pennsylvania
15 Pa. C. S. A. § 1709

(a) Presiding officer.- There shall be a presiding officer at every meeting of the shareholders. The presiding officer shall be appointed in the manner provided in the bylaws or, in the absence of such provision, by the board of directors. If the bylaws are silent on the appointment of the presiding officer and the board fails to designate a presiding officer, the president shall be the presiding officer.

(b) Authority of the presiding officer.- Except as otherwise provided in the bylaws, the presiding officer shall determine the order of business and shall have the authority to establish rules for the conduct of the meeting.

(c) Procedural standard.- Any action by the presiding officer in adopting rules for and in conducting a meeting shall be fair to the shareholders.

(d) Closing of the polls.- The presiding officer shall announce at the meeting when the polls close for each matter voted upon. If no announcement is made, the polls shall be deemed to have closed upon the final adjournment of the meeting. After the polls close, no ballots, proxies or votes, nor any revocations or changes thereto, may be accepted.

ADJOURNMENT OF A BOARD MEETING

Pennsylvania
15 Pa. C. S. A. § 1755

TIME OF HOLDING MEETINGS OF SHAREHOLDERS

[See statute for other provisions on regular and special meetings.]

(b) Special meetings.- Special meetings of the shareholders may be called at any time:

(1) by the board of directors;

(2) unless otherwise provided in the articles, by shareholders entitled to cast at least 20% of the votes that all shareholders are entitled to cast at the particular meeting; or

(3) by such officers or other persons as may be provided in the bylaws.

At any time, upon written request of any person who has called a special meeting, it shall be the duty of the secretary to fix the time of the meeting which, if the meeting is called pursuant to a statutory right, shall be held not more than 60 days after the receipt of the request. If the secretary neglects or refuses to fix the time of the meeting, the person or persons calling the meeting may do so. See section 2521 (relating to call of special meetings of shareholders).

(c) **Adjournments.**- Adjournments of any regular or special meeting may be taken but any meeting at which directors are to be elected shall be adjourned only from day to day, or for such longer periods not exceeding 15 days each as the shareholders present and entitled to vote shall direct, until the directors have been elected. See section 2522 (relating to adjournment of meetings of shareholders).

[See Pa. statute for other provisions regarding regular and special meetings of shareholders.]

MANNER OF GIVING NOTICE

Pennsylvania
15 Pa. C. S. A. § 1702

[See statute for all provisions.]

(b) **Adjourned shareholder meetings.**- When a meeting of shareholders is adjourned, it shall not be necessary to give any notice of the adjourned meeting or of the business to be transacted at an adjourned meeting, other than by announcement at the meeting at which the adjournment is taken, unless the board fixes a new record date for the adjourned meeting or this subpart requires notice of the business to be transacted and such notice has not previously been given.

VOTING RIGHTS OF SHAREHOLDERS

Pennsylvania
15 Pa. C. S. A. § 1758

[See statute for other provisions on shareholder voting.]

(b) Procedures for elections of directors.- Unless otherwise restricted in the bylaws, in elections for directors, voting need not be by ballot unless required by vote of the shareholders before the voting for election of directors begins. The candidates for election as directors receiving the highest number of votes from each class or group of classes, if any, entitled to elect directors separately up to the number of directors to be elected by the class or group of classes shall be elected. If at any meeting of shareholders, directors of more than one class are to be elected, each class of directors shall be elected in a separate election.

SELECTION OF DIRECTORS

Pennsylvania
a. C. S. A. § 1725 (b)

(a) General rule.- Except as otherwise provided in this section, directors of a business corporation, other than those constituting the first board of directors, shall be elected by the shareholders. A bylaw adopted by the shareholders may classify the directors with respect to the shareholders who exercise the power to elect directors.

[See statute for other provisions on selection of directors.]

(b) Vacancies.-.

(1) Except as otherwise provided in the bylaws:

(i) Vacancies in the board of directors, including vacancies resulting from an increase in the number of directors, may be filled by a majority vote of the remaining members of the board though less than a quorum, or by a sole remaining director, and each person so selected shall be a director to serve for the balance of the unexpired term unless otherwise restricted in the bylaws.

(ii) When one or more directors resign from the board effective at a future date, the directors then in office, including those who have so resigned, shall have power by the applicable vote to fill the vacancies, the vote thereon to take effect when the resignations become effective.

REMOVAL OF DIRECTORS BY SHAREHOLDERS

Pennsylvania
15 Pa. C. S. A. § 1726 (a)

§1726.- **Removal of directors**

[See Pa. statute for other provisions on removal by the board and by the court.]

(a) Removal by the shareholders.-

(1) Unless otherwise provided in a bylaw adopted by the shareholders, the entire board of directors, or a class of the board where the board is classified with respect to the power to select directors, or any individual director of a business corporation may be removed from office without assigning any cause by the vote of shareholders, or of the holders of a class or series of shares, entitled to elect directors, or the class of directors. In case the board or a class of the board or any one or more directors are so removed, new directors may be elected at the same meeting. Notwithstanding the first sentence of this paragraph, unless otherwise provided in the articles by a specific and unambiguous statement that directors may be removed from

office without assigning any cause, the entire board of directors, or any class of the board, or any individual director of a corporation having a board classified as permitted by section 1724(b) (relating to classified board of directors), may be removed from office by vote of the shareholders entitled to vote thereon only for cause, if such classification has been effected in the articles or by a bylaw adopted by the shareholders.

(2) The repeal of a provision of the articles or bylaws prohibiting, or the addition of a provision to the articles or bylaws permitting, the removal by the shareholders of the board, a class of the board or a director without assigning any cause shall not apply to any incumbent director during the balance of the term for which he was selected.

(3) An individual director shall not be removed (unless the entire board or class of the board is removed) from the board of a corporation in which shareholders are entitled to vote cumulatively for the board or a class of the board if sufficient votes are cast against the resolution for his removal which, if cumulatively voted at any annual or other regular election of directors, would be sufficient to elect one or more directors to the board or to the class.

(4) The board of directors may be removed at any time with or without cause by the unanimous vote or consent of shareholders entitled to vote thereon.

(5) The articles may not prohibit the removal of directors by the shareholders for cause.

DIRECTOR DISSENT AT A MEETING

Pennsylvania
15 Pa. C. S. A. § 514

§ 514.- Notation of dissent

A director of a domestic corporation who is present at a meeting of its board of directors, or of a committee of the board, at which action on any corporate matter is taken on which the director is generally competent to act, shall be presumed to have assented to the action taken unless his dissent is entered in the minutes of the meeting or unless he files his written dissent to the action with the secretary of the meeting before the adjournment thereof or transmits the dissent in writing to the secretary of the corporation immediately after the adjournment of the meeting. The right to dissent shall not apply to a director who voted in favor of the action. Nothing in this sub-chapter shall bar a director from asserting that minutes of the meeting incorrectly omitted his dissent if, promptly upon receipt of a copy of such minutes, he notifies the secretary in writing of the asserted omission or inaccuracy.

JUDGES OF ELECTION

Pennsylvania
15 Pa. C. S. A. § 1765

§ 1765. Judges of election

(a) General rule.- Unless otherwise provided in a bylaw adopted by the shareholders:

(1) Appointment.- In advance of any meeting of shareholders of a business corporation, the board of directors may appoint judges of election, who need not be shareholders, to act at the meeting or any adjournment thereof. If judges of election are not so appointed, the presiding officer of the meeting may, and on the request of any shareholder shall, appoint judges of election at the meeting. The number of judges shall be one or three. A person who is a candidate for office to be filled at the meeting shall not act as a judge.

(2) Vacancies.- In case any person appointed as a judge fails to appear or fails or refuses to act, the vacancy may be filled by appointment made by the board of directors in advance of the convening of the meeting or at the meeting by the presiding officer thereof.

(3) Duties.- The judges of election shall determine the number of shares outstanding and the voting power of each, the shares represented at the meeting, the existence of a quorum, the authenticity, validity and effect of proxies, receive votes or ballots, hear and determine all challenges and questions in any way arising in connection with the right to vote, count and tabulate all votes, determine the result and do such acts as may be proper to conduct the election or vote with fairness to all shareholders. The judges of election shall perform their duties impartially, in good faith, to the best of their ability and as expeditiously as is practical. If there are three judges of election, the decision, act or certificate of a majority shall be effective in all respects as the decision, act or certificate of all.

(4) Report.- On request of the presiding officer of the meeting, or of any shareholder, the judges shall make a report in writing of any challenge or question or matter determined by them, and execute a certificate of any fact found by them. Any report or certificate made by them shall be prima facie evidence of the facts stated therein.

AMEND BYLAWS - SHAREHOLDERS QUORUM OR VOTING REQUIREMENTS

AMENDMENT OF BYLAWS

Pennsylvania
15 Pa. C. S. A. § 1504 (a)

§ 1504. Adoption, amendment and contents of bylaws

[See Pa. statute for other provisions on this subject.]

(a) General rule.- Except as otherwise provided in this subpart, the shareholders entitled to vote shall have the power to adopt, amend and repeal the bylaws of a business corporation. Except as provided in subsection (b), the authority to adopt, amend and repeal bylaws may be expressly vested by the bylaws in the board of directors, subject to the power of the shareholders to change such action. The bylaws may contain any provision for managing the business and regulating the affairs of the corporation not inconsistent with law or the articles. In the case of a meeting of shareholders, written notice shall be given to each shareholder that the purpose, or one of the purposes, of a meeting is to consider the adoption, amendment or repeal of the bylaws. There shall be included in, or enclosed with, the notice a copy of the proposed amendment or a summary of the changes to e effected thereby. Any change in the bylaws shall take effect when adopted unless otherwise provided in the resolution effecting the change.

INDEMNIFICATION

Pennsylvania
15 Pa. C. S. A. § 1744

§ 1744. Procedure for effecting indemnification

Unless ordered by a court, any indemnification under section 1741 (relating to third-party actions) or 1742 (relating to derivative and corporate actions) shall be made by the business corporation only as authorized in the specific case upon a determination that indemnification of the representative is proper in the circumstances because he has met the applicable standard of conduct set forth in those sections. The determination shall be made:

(1) by the board of directors by a majority vote of a quorum consisting of directors who were not parties to the action or proceeding;

(2) if such a quorum is not obtainable or if obtainable and a majority vote of a quorum of disinterested directors so directs, by independent legal counsel in a written opinion; or

(3) by the shareholders.

Index of Subjects

(References are to section numbers)

Challenges
   to vote or election, § 21
Changing a vote, § 31
Closed meetings, § 5, 12
Closing of polls, § 3, 31
Committees
   generally, § 5, 6
   nominations by, § 32
Conflict of interest of director of organization, § 5, 13, 36, 47
Consent, voting by general, § 18, 24, 28, 42, 44
Contested elections, § 32
Courts

D
Debate
   generally, § 2, 3, 4, 17, 18, 31
Departure of participant, effect on quorum, § 15
Directors of organization
   generally, § 1
   accepting the position, § 32
   amendment, powers of, § 33
   authority vis-à-vis shareholders, § 33, 37
   conflict of interest, § 5
   duties, § 1, 11
   indemnification, § 46
   meetings, generally, § 1, 2, 13, 17, 18, 19, 20, 21, 22, 24, 31
   powers, § 37, 39
   removal and resignation, § 40, 41, 42, 43, 44, 45
   selection and qualification, § 32
   vacancies, § 13
   waiver of improper notice, § 20
Dissent regarding notice
   right of director in minutes, §20
   waiver of right to, §20
Dissolution of organization, § 28
Due process
   removal of directors, § 42, 43, 44

E
Elections
   generally, § 3, 32, 34, 35, 42
   challenges to election, § 32
   contested, § 32
   courts, § 1, 35, 37
   directors, election of, § 32
   inspectors of elections, §32
   necessary vote to elect, § 32

About the Author

Harry S. Rosenthal, JD, PRP, is a lawyer and parliamentarian located in the Philadelphia, Pennsylvania, area. He has been a member of the National Association of Parliamentarians for over twenty years and has attained the status of Professional Registered Parliamentarian. A member of the Pennsylvania Bar, Mr. Rosenthal holds a juris doctor degree from Temple University School of Law. He has served as a professional parliamentarian for many national organizations and has written numerous articles on the subject. He has also authored a companion book entitled *Parliamentary Law and Practice for Nonprofit Organizations - Third Edition* (Amazon Books). He may be contacted at Lawhsr@gmail.com or through his website, www. ParliamentaryServices.US.

A VALUABLE MEETING AND PROCEDURAL REFERENCE FOR BUSINESS CORPORATIONS, BOARDS, AND SHAREHOLDERS

This handy and valuable procedural reference book bridges a large informational gap for those who are preparing for, leading, and attending board of directors and shareholders business corporation meetings. The author simultaneously draws upon the three principal sources of meeting authority on the subject by including

- a sample of state for-profit statutory law,
- selected case law, and
- for added perspective, two of the principal parliamentary rule books.

This unique book combines the relationship between traditional parliamentary procedure with other legally based meeting procedures used by corporate boards and shareholders. Information about procedures for indemnification of directors, the importance of meeting minutes, and the use of executive (closed) sessions is also provided. It is vital for corporations to stay informed on these subjects. *Meeting Practice and Procedure for Business Corporations: Boards and Shareholders* is a practical and authoritative resource for those who govern and participate in formal meetings of business organizations—such as officers, directors, shareholders, corporate officials, and their staff.

Harry S. Rosenthal is a practicing attorney and a professional parliamentarian recognized by the National Association of Parliamentarians. Based in the Philadelphia area, Mr. Rosenthal has served as a parliamentarian for many national organizations. He has also authored numerous articles on the topic of parliamentary procedure. He is author of the companion book *Parliamentary Law and Practice for Nonprofit Organizations – Third Edition.* Mr. Rosenthal can be contacted at Lawhsr@gmail.com and through his website: www.ParliamentaryServices.US.